Leccister, May '87

# The Future of Democracy

# NORBERTO BOBBIO

# The Future of Democracy
*A Defence of the
Rules of the Game*

*Translated by Roger Griffin
Edited and introduced by Richard Bellamy*

Polity Press

This translation first published 1987 by Polity Press
in association with Basil Blackwell.

Editorial Office: Polity Press, Dales Brewery, Gwydir Street, Cambridge CB1 2LJ, UK

Basil Blackwell Ltd
108 Cowley Road, Oxford OX4 1JF, UK

**British Library Cataloguing in Publication Data**

Bobbio, Norberto
  The future of democracy.
  1. Democracy
  I. Title    II. Il futuro della democrazia.
  English
  321.8    JC423
  ISBN 0-7456-0308-4
  ISBN 0-7456-0309-2 Pbk

Typeset by Joshua Associates Limited, Oxford
Printed in Great Britain by Billing and Sons Ltd Worcester

# Contents

# Introduction

Most regimes today regard themselves as either democratic or as moving towards the establishment of democracy. This universal praise of democracy has produced considerable confusion in the use of the concept, since large differences clearly exist between these self-styled democractic political systems. The divergences in the practices of putative democracies have led to theoretical debate about the term's conceptual coherence and created a gulf between descriptive and prescriptive characterizations of democratic practice in the work of political scientists and political theorists respectively. Whereas the former argue that we must adapt our aspirations to the conditions of modern politics and modify our theory of democracy accordingly, the latter deny that empirical evidence can ever force changes in theories which are largely normative.[1] It is a great merit of Bobbio's book to have bridged this divide successfully by combining an historically sensitive analysis of democracy's substantive meaning with a sociologically aware discussion of the political implications of adopting a particular definition. This fruitful combination of history with social and political theory enables him to follow his examination of the values attributed to democracy with a number of suggestions about how democratic practice might be extended in the future. He therefore performs an important service not only to his fellow scholars but equally to his fellow citizens. For an awareness of the shortcomings of existing democracies, and of the deficiencies of and discrepancies between theorists of democracy, has a tendency to provoke disillusionment with the democratic idea itself, and to lead to its dismissal as fundamentally incoherent and impractical. The survival of democracy as a political form depends upon studies such as Bobbio's, which unite an account of the ideals of democracy with the specification of the institutional framework best suited to their realization, and which offer a justification of the preference for one model over others. By providing a plausible future for democracy, Bobbio has contributed to ensuring that it will have one.

Bobbio's book is sufficiently clear to stand on its own, without a lengthy introduction. However, since his work is largely unknown to the English-speaking public, and initially addressed to an Italian audience, some preliminary context setting may be helpful. I shall therefore give a few details concerning the intellectual and political orientation of his thought, and then outline his argument briefly, drawing attention to the contribution it makes to current debates in the Anglo-American literature.

I

Norberto Bobbio was born in Turin in 1909. The cultural and social environment of his native city has a special importance in explaining Bobbio's intellectual and ideological allegiances. During the 1920s and 1930s the university continued to be a stronghold of the Italian liberal empiricist tradition, and as such something of an anomaly during the heyday of Crocean idealism and its left-wing (Gramscian/ communist) and right-wing (Gentilian/fascist) variants.[2] Teachers such as the economist Luigi Einaudi, the political scientist Gaetano Mosca and Bobbio's professor, the legal philosopher Gioele Solari, bred an unfashionable distrust of metaphysical political systems amongst their students, combined with a critical regard for the liberal institutions of the market and parliamentary democracy. These ideological choices, unusual at a time when both fascists and their opponents were united in their condemnation of the earlier Giolittian regime, were reinforced by the peculiar social and political situation in Turin. We have become accustomed to associating the relatively advanced industrial and class structure of this city with Gramsci's theory of proletarian revolution. However, it also spawned a very different and more approving appreciation of the benefits of capital- ism. Gramscian communism had to compete with, and was chal- lenged by, radical liberal and reformist socialist alternatives, which, whilst accepting the need for social change, were critical of the Marxist programme. This tradition gave rise to an influential non- communist anti-fascist movement initially centred on the Turin periodical *La Rivoluzione Liberale* (*The Liberal Revolution*) and later identified with the movement Giustizia e Libertà (Justice and Liberty), inspired by the ideas of Carlo Rosselli.[3]

Rosselli contended that the Marxist attribution of a complete opposition between liberalism and socialism was mistaken. Many of his criticisms hit the straw man of the vulgar scientific Marxism of the time, and his arguments concerning the incompatibility of individual freedom and historical determinism appear too crude as a result. More lasting, however, is the conclusion he drew from his analysis, namely, that Marxists had insufficiently addressed the problem of individual autonomy, essential to liberalism. Whilst Marxism correctly regarded social and economic reform as necessary pre-conditions for the liberation of the proletariat, this in itself did not guarantee the civil liberties of individuals after the revolution.[4] Socialism, in Rosselli's view, was distinguished from communism by its insistence that 'the process of elevating the masses and the reform of social relations on the basis of a principle of justice is brought into harmony with the liberty of individuals and of groups.'[5] Socialism must achieve its goals by 'the liberal method', the institutional framework of liberal democracy.[6]

The fascist and Stalinist regimes of the time had persuaded Rosselli and his followers that it was the liberal rather than the capitalist or communist character of a regime which was decisive in preserving basic political liberties. Moreover, fascism convinced them of the inadequacy of mere mass participation in elections as an adequate defence against authoritarianism.[7] Political education had always been a central problem for Italian intellectuals, and a party system on the elitist model was seen as a possible solution. As Bobbio has pointed out, the theory of elites never formed part of the official doctrine of fascism. Contrary to a popular misconception, democratic writers such as Gobetti and Guido Dorso were far more interested in developing it.[8] Bobbio himself has played an important role in reviving this tradition of Italian thought, and has produced new editions of the works of Mosca and Pareto.[9] In advocating this doctrine of liberal socialism, which combined the three elements of constitutionalism, parliamentarism, and a competitive multi-party system, Italian theorists were very much influenced by the ideas and experience of English 'new liberals' and socialists within the Labour Party.[10] As Rosselli and others pointed out, the survival of demo-cracy and the fate of the working class there was in marked contrast to events in both Italy and Russia.[11]

Bobbio's work continues the project of this movement to recon-cile the demands of social justice with individual civil and political liberty. The vast bulk of recent commentaries on Italian politics have been concerned with exploring the Italian Communist Party's claim to provide a 'third way' for the development of Western polities, distinct from either liberal capitalism or state socialism. This proposal hinges on a radical theory of democracy, stemming from

4 INTRODUCTION

Gramsci, and the role it would play in a communist society involving collective ownership of the means of production.[12] The Italian Socialist Party, to which Bobbio belongs, has long distanced itself from this programme. In an earlier work, *What is Socialism?* (1976), Bobbio offered a number of trenchant criticisms of Marxism, and in particular of the belief that notions of justice and rights are products of the bourgeois capitalist system and would be redundant under communism.[13] Drawing on the arguments of Marx and Lenin,[14] Marxists have argued that once class divisions are abolished through the suppression of private property then the 'bourgeois liberties' protecting the integrity of the individual will be redundant. The interests of all members of society will ultimately be compatible with each other. In the interim a revolutionary party, speaking for the as yet unarticulated interests of the proletariat, can legitimately assume power. Yet, as the disastrous political record of actually existing socialist countries has demonstrated, this theory has in practice simply involved placing power in a far more coherent and self-serving governing elite than has ever existed in liberal regimes. A constitutional lawyer by training, Bobbio has stressed the need for a political and legal framework capable of preserving the rights of individuals to choose their representatives freely. In the present book he develops these arguments and mounts a detailed attack on various models of direct democracy. However, he also sketches an alternative of his own, whereby he aims to show that socialist goals can only be achieved acceptably within the liberal democratic institutional framework.

II

The manifest shortcomings of liberal democratic states have induced many critics on the left to insist on the need for a profound transformation of the economy as both a necessary and sufficient condition for 'true' democracy to emerge. However, the experience of actually existing socialist states casts serious doubt on this claim. Bobbio, in contrast, shows that the left must take the criticisms and proposals of liberal thinkers seriously if it is to provide a workable alternative of its own. Without in any way diminishing the deficiencies of western democracies and their apologists, he argues that not only the formal liberal civil and political rights but the whole constitutional and institutional framework of liberal democracies as well are essential for democracy. According to Bobbio, liberal democracy is not a contradiction in terms, as Marxists have maintained, but more nearly a tautology. For 'if liberalism provides those liberties necessary for the proper exercise of democratic power, democracy guarantees the existence and persistence of fundamental liberties.'[15] He adopts a minimal definition of democracy as 'a set of rules ... which establish *who* is authorised to take collective decisions and which *procedures* are to be used to choose them'.[16] These rules consist of the majority principle – that is, decisions are made by a simple majority vote – and a number of civil and political rights, to freedom of speech and association and one vote per citizen, which guarantee rough political equality between voters and a choice between real alternatives at elections.

Bobbio follows theorists such as Schumpeter,[17] Dahl[18] and Sartori[19] in arguing that these requirements are best satisfied by the competitive model of different parties vying for the people's vote, rather than by the classical model of participatory democracy.[20] Bobbio gives four main reasons for this. First, the modern ethos is individualistic, so that no amount of rational argument will bring about an all-embracing general will. Second, this cultural orientation is reinforced by the diversification of modern industrial society, which makes it harder to form common interests. Third, direct democracy could not mean that we vote on each and every issue after a prolonged discussion of all the elements involved – there simply would not be enough hours in the day. The only solution would be to mandate delegates to vote in specified ways. The difficulty here is that we belong to too many diverse groups – for example as workers, parents, city dwellers, etc. – for this not to either shade into the competitive model by degrees, or result in the false attribution of certain 'real interests' to the people as a whole. Finally, the increased complexity of modern society makes people ill-informed judges of their own interests, so that representatives can serve us better than we can ourselves.

Bobbio believes the competitive model is better suited to the pluralist nature of modern society. Its chief advantages are instrumental. He contends that political experts are likely to produce more effective policies than a badly informed populace. Moreover, the competitive model is more efficient that the participatory alternatives in turning votes into policies. One of the inherent problems of majority decisions is that certain minorities with intense preferences for a particular good may be consistently outvoted. Classical theorists claimed that the educative effects of the decision/making process would modify the majority's view to take the intensity of minority feeling into account. But this effect is only likely to obtain in small communities, where each person can take part in the making of important decisions and hear and be influenced by the opinions of everyone else. In contrast, advocates of the competitive party system assert that the pluralistic nature of modern society makes it inevitable that any majority will have to be made up of a number of minorities. Parties will therefore have to produce platforms which accord due weight to minority opinion and co-ordinate compromises and trade-offs on the voters' behalf.[21]

This latter solution does not give complete satisfaction, however, and Bobbio carefully enumerates the inadequacies of the competitive party model, and frequently refers to the failings of contemporary Italy to illustrate his criticisms. For example, in a two-party system the competition between parties may well lead to a movement to the middle ground, where most votes are to be found, and the exclusion of radical alternatives. Parties will deliberately seek to project a moderate image and shed ideological extremists. The electoral advantages of this strategy, for instance, has been a constant problem for the British Labour Party, dividing the leadership from many of its most ardent supporters. The same pressures to dilute ideology do not occur in a multi-party system, such as the Italian. In this instance, the parties will have the opposite incentive and stress ideological differences. Here the drawback is that no one party is likely to gain an overall majority and hence be totally responsible for implementing its manifesto. This fact makes government policy less accountable to the electorate. The ruling parties can always claim that the other coalition partners forced them to back down on their declared programme and that rescuing parts of it was better than it not being implemented at all. Finally, leaders of parties may identify more with each other in certain crucial respects than with those they represent. This circumstance could result in their colluding with each other in order to keep certain issues off the political agenda. They form a 'political class', to use Mosca's term, with common interests as actual or potential rulers.[22] Ever since unification Italy has been governed by an elite group which has sacrificed ideological differences for the shared spoils of power. Even though the widening of the franchise has changed matters in significant ways, the clientelistic nature of politics continues to hinder the democratic control of government.

Since the Second World War Italian political parties have obtained a great deal of patronage through their control of numerous state monopolies and quangos. None of this power is directly accountable to the electorate. The major parliamentary parties divide these positions up according to considerations dictated by the exigencies of forming coalitions or the need to obtain tacit consent for their programmes, so that certain groups gain an influence far beyond their electoral support. Their control of essential services is so extensive that the system has come to be known as 'subterranean government' or *sottogoverno*. Yet it is unlikely to be reformed, since all parties have a common interest in this system, which gives them the resources to offer their members numerous incentives for continuing their support beyond success at the polls or the implementation of their declared programme.[23]

During the 1950s, pluralists such as Dahl tended to minimize these difficulties. Dahl argued that the 'polyarchical' nature of contemporary society rendered the liberal fear of the 'tyranny of the majority' a chimera, since only 'minorities' could rule, not a single majority. This system overcomes the problem of weighing the intensity of preferences by ensuring that 'all the active and legitimate groups in the population can make themselves heard at some crucial stage in the process of decision.'[24] Two assumptions underlay this thesis. First, he maintained that 'social training' through the family, schools, newspapers, etc., produced a basic consensus on norms and values amongst at least the political leaders.[25] Second, he believed that political activity is a function of relative intensity.[26] The more a group feels about an issue, the greater will be its activism in promoting it. However, both of these presuppositions seem empirically dubious. Differences in organizational skills, education and finances will give certain groups, for example big business, greater advantages than others can muster. Underprivileged groups, such as racial minorities or the poor, lack the resources to sustain an organization. They can only offer the distant hope of eventual success to maintain their support, whereas wealthier concerns, or ones that are better positioned socially, can offer a host of immediate short-term benefits to their members. Thus a polluting chemical plant can use its monopoly of local employment opportunities to undermine the case of environmentalists complaining of long-term damage. Unions can give their members extensive immediate private benefits, but an association of the unemployed cannot firm up support in this way, even if it would be in the long-term collective interest of the jobless to join.[27] In addition, organizations such as corporations and bureaucracies can wield a subtle and coercive power over the choices voters make. Not only do they have more lobbying influence than the individual citizen, but they may actually control the circumstances in which votes are made by limiting the available alternatives through their monopoly of employment opportunities, credit facilities, knowledge and expertise in particular areas, etc. These are 'invisible powers', to use Bobbio's suggestive term, undermining democratic practices.[28]

The existence of these social and economic inequalities erodes in turn the citizen's allegiance to shared social values, on which Dahl counts. Greater wealth not only gives certain individuals or groups greater influence in the choosing and influencing of candidates and issues, but also means that they are not necessarily affected equally by the results of democratic decisions they dislike. Fines, for example, fall disproportionately on the rich and the poor. This produces cynicism on the part of the relatively powerless and encourages the self-interested 'free riding' of those with power. In Italy, as Bobbio notes, the position has degenerated even further with the presence of organized criminal elements in the south, which use violence to obtain electoral support or stifle the opposition.[29]

The weaknesses of existing democracies are thus all too evident to Italian observers, and have contributed to what Bobbio calls the 'broken promises' of democracy. Democracy has not lived up to the expectations of its early proponents, and failed to eliminate the additional influence in decision making afforded to certain individuals due to inequalities of wealth, power and knowledge, or even to inculcate a heightened political awareness and/or increase of civic virtue among the newly enfranchised masses. As a result, Bobbio retains a healthy scepticism about regarding democracy pure and simple as the panacea of all political ills.

Radicals, however, often argue as if these difficulties could be solved simply by extending democracy to cover practically all decision making. We have already noted some of the drawbacks of this idea, such as the almost limitless inflation of political activity and the problem of insuffcent knowledge amongst the electorate. A variation of this scheme is to have more participatory democracy in areas which are sufficiently well defined for its virtues to be realized, such as in the workplace and local government. This proposal has always appealed to socialist pluralists, such as G. D. H. Cole[30] and H. J. Laski[31] and their ideas were much admired by the Italian liberal socialists. More recently advocates of participatory democracy, such as Carole Pateman[32] and Peter Bachrach,[33] have turned to this tradition for inspiration. Gramsci's support for 'factory councils' has also been assimilated to this line of thought.[34]

Bobbio points out two defects to this approach. First, unless one believes absolutely in the educative nature of political participation, then the mere extension of democracy in this way will not necessarily produce any better results. After all, even on small committees intense minorities can be consistently denied an effective voice by the majority. Second, advocates of this devolved form of participation assert that it strengthens the links between the individual and national politics; that participation at the local level prepares the citizen for informed involvement outside this sphere. However, this claim is in contradiction with a further assumption of socialist pluralists, namely that equal weight can be given to different interest groups by virtue of allowing them to be as self-managing as possible. They argue that the best way of strengthening the liberal freedoms of speech and association, so that they reflect social and economic reality, is to return to workers, etc., authority over their own lives in the various spheres in which they move. The problem with this proposal is that it has a tendency to exacerbate, rather than diminish, the conflicts between groups by strengthening group identity. The decisions made in industry are more specialized than in national politics. The latter is concerned with the aggregation of policy preferences and values and only subordinately with technique and the interests of specialized functions. In industry, however, these become of prime importance. Whilst the nation is a largely inclusive community, involving all the relevant parties, workplace democracy cannot include all those affected by its decisions, such as consumers, workers' dependents, other factories, etc.[35] The guild socialists and Gramsci circumvented these difficulties by assuming that a natural organic harmony existed between different economic functions, and that a heightened perception of the mutually beneficial interrelations between society's diverse parts would reduce conflict. As Bobbio remarks, this is the pluralism of a feudal rather than a democratic society. Moreover, it fails to go much beyond the thesis of liberal pluralists; indeed Dahl in his recent work has essentially espoused a very similar theory.[36] As a result, all the attendant difficulties of the polyarchal view, outlined above, remain.[37]

Bobbio's vision of a possible future for democracy attempts to avoid the pitfalls of these various models. He addresses the two main issues raised by modern theorists:

(a)  the need to extend democratic control to a number of areas within society in a practical manner, and
(b)  to ensure that political equality consists of more than the formal entitlement of one vote per citizen.

He traces the difficulties of democratic theorists in meeting these two needs to certain tensions within liberalism. Traditionally socialists have tried to circumvent these problems by simply rejecting the liberal heritage altogether; Bobbio, however, engages directly with it. Liberalism originated, in Bobbio's account, as a political reaction to authoritarian government in early modern Europe. Its main concern was to grant individuals civil liberties against the incursion of the state. This origin produced an ambiguity in the liberal attitude towards democracy. As a procedure it provides a means of legitimizing a government by formally requesting the consent of all citizens. However a number of problems arise immediately. For example, have those who did not vote at all, because they dislike all the opinions, given their consent? Should all opinions be weighed equally in any case? Liberalism has tended to avoid such questions by keeping the state's functions to a minimum and stressing the autonomy of society. Social processes are seen as essentially unplanned and hence fair, reflecting the merit and effort of the individuals involved. However this view begins to come into conflict with democratic political ideals. For the latter seem to require a different sort of equality, based on need or our common humanity.[38]

In addressing this question, Bobbio examines the ideas of J. S. Mill and the new contractarians. Mill reveals the ambivalence of the liberal position in paradigmatic fashion. Whilst he undoubtedly believed all should have equal civil rights, he was deeply suspicious about extending the franchise to include the propertyless and uneducated. His advocacy of plural votes for the better educated was perfectly in keeping with the liberal belief that the rewards of politics, like those of the market, should go to those who deserved them. Thus although he approved of equality of opportunity, and hence opposed the unearned privilege of inherited wealth, or discrimination on grounds of sex, creed or colour, this did not extend to a commitment to giving everyone an equal say in government – quite the reverse.[39]

Even in Mill's time this was not an entirely satisfactory stance to take. We have already rehearsed the problems social and economic inequalities raise for modern democrats. Yet even within classical liberalism a dissonance was noted between the need for economic independence when voting and the impossibility of achieving this as long as some members of the community were subservient to others for their livelihood.[40] Meeting the claims of democracy, however, has not proved universally acceptable to those of liberal sentiments. Some have argued that the cost is too high, that the demands of individuals upon the resources of their fellow citizens for more welfare, better schooling and hospitals, etc., 'overloads' government beyond its capacity to pay for such schemes.[41] Others go further, they invoke the traditional liberal antipathy to government and insist on the inviolability of the individual against external interference. In recent theories, such as Nozick's, neo-liberal or libertarian thinkers have argued that defending individual liberty entails an entitlement right to the products of our labour or skill in the market which makes taxation an infringement of the integrity of the individual similar to physical coercion.[42] Bobbio contests the comparison, pointing out that liberal rights against the state were asserted with a view to curbing the powers of hereditary monarchs, not elected governments. The theory also sets the limits to state interference impossibly high. Most libertarians accept that a minimal state will be needed to enforce recognition of the contractual rights and duties basic to the free market economy. But if taxation is equivalent to coercion how is this to be funded? They would appear to be hoist with their own petard.[43]

Bobbio argues that in spite of these contradictions within liberalism we cannot ignore it or even reject it outright. Despite the disconcertingly reactionary character of many of its new forms, liberalism continues to thrive 'because', Bobbio writes, 'it is rooted in a philosophical outlook which, like it or not, gave birth to the modern world: the individualistic conception of society and history.'[44] He berates the left for never having come to terms with this conception. Apart from anarchism, it has tended to advocate 'organic' views of community which regard the individual as a mere part of greater whole, and has accordingly produced schemes for functional rather than individual representation. Bobbio criticizes this line of reasoning as regressive and unsuited to the conditions of modern society. Today, 'the starting point for every scheme for human emancipation is the individual with his *passions* (to be channelled or tamed), his *interests* (to be regulated and coordinated), and with his *needs* (to be satisfied or repressed).'[45] He contends that the contractarian tradition provides the best foundation for establishing agreements in an individualist society, and points to the proliferation of contractual obligations within modern societies, not only for the purposes of commercial exchanges, but also between governments and citizens – as in union pay and strike agreements – and even between governments in foreign treaties. A contractual arrangement, within the liberal tradition of Hobbes, Locke and Kant, represents a procedure whereby all interested parties may consent freely to a given social set-up and make trade-offs of certain personal liberties for the greater advantages they feel will derive from it. As a result, it is well suited to the pluralist and individualist nature of the modern world, since it forms an uncontentious basis for our social and political obligations without sacrificing individual liberty. The task for the democratic left, therefore,

is to see whether, starting with the same incontestable individualist conception of society and using the same institutional structures, we are able to make a counter-proposal to the theory of social contract which neo-liberals want to put into operation; one which would include in its conditions a principle of distributive justice and which would hence be compatible with the theoretical and practical tradition of socialism.[46]

Bobbio believes that John Rawls has designed such a new type of social contract, one capable of underpinning the equality of status required by members of the modern democratic polity.[47]

Since Bobbio does not go into the details of Rawls's argument, I shall describe it here briefly. I will draw on Rawls's most recent statement of his position,[48] as I believe this comes nearer to Bobbio's interpretation than the earlier *A Theory of Justice* did. Rawls maintains that 'the public culture of a democratic society' is committed to seeking forms of social co-operation which can be pursued on a basis of mutual respect between free and equal persons.[49] This co-operation does not imply the co-ordination of social activity by an outside agency, but simply involves the acceptance of certain common procedures to regulate political conduct. However, he adds it must also contain fair terms specifying the basic rights and duties of citizens within society, so that the benefits produced by everyone's efforts are distributed fairly between generations over time.[50] Rawls argues that we can arrive at such a scheme via a process of 'reflective equilibrium', whereby we abstract from our present situation and arrive by philosophical meditation at the substantive basis of our political and moral convictions.[51]

He adopts the device of a hypothetical 'original position' to arrive at two principles of justice which he believes agents would choose freely if they were ignorant of their present abilities and social position as fair for society as a whole.[52] According to his latest formulation these are:

1    Each person has an equal right to a fully adequate scheme of equal basic rights and liberties, which scheme is compatible with a similar scheme for all.

2    Social and economic inequalities are to satisfy, two conditions: first, they must be attached to offices and positions open to all under conditions of fair equality of opportunity; and second, they must be to the greatest benefit of the least advantaged members of society.[53]

The two principles are 'lexically ordered', so that the first takes priority over the second and 2(i) has precedence over 2(ii). Together they aim to meet and harmonize the respective claims of liberty and equality in modern democratic societies.[54]

In Rawls's view this goal entails that citizens be accorded equal respect in the pursuit of their idea of the good.[55] As the recent literature has stressed,[56] and Rawls now admits,[57] his theory assumes a particular type of agent possessing a sense of justice and a capacity to conceive a conception of the good. His ideal polity would also rule out those individuals who believed that their personal conception of the good involved enforcing others to abide by it too. Thus, for example, whilst he does not exclude religious groups who require strict conformity from their members, he could not countenance the formation of a theocratic state. The theory of justice forms, in his view, an 'overlapping consensus' between different groups and individuals with divergent beliefs and life-styles as to the fair procedures for making political demands in a democratic society, where mutual toleration and fairness must be the norm.[58]

Numerous criticisms have been made of Rawls's theory concerning the viability of his derivation of the principles from the original position and the conception of social justice he espouses. These need not concern us here.[59] The appeal of the Rawlsian project to Bobbio is that his notion of 'pure procedural justice' appears to undercut the popular notion that the market mechanism of unplanned outcomes rewarding the abilities people prefer is intrinsically fairer than any other system. Whatever its defects, Rawls's theory purports to demonstrate that showing people equal respect entails according them social and political as well as civil rights. In particular, Rawls's idea of a new type of social contract as the basis for a democratic society provides Bobbio with the framework for the consensual norms he requires for his proposed extension of democratic practices.[60]

According to Bobbio, the main issue for democrats today is not 'who can vote?' but 'where can you vote?'[61] The ideal of democracy involves the notion that we are free only when we have chosen the decisions which bind us from a range of valid alternatives and without the restraint or coercion of others. Meeting this requirement means granting not only equal civil and political rights but social rights as well. However a further difficulty with modern democracy stems from the diversification and specialization of contemporary life, which has produced the growth of numerous agencies outside our control – bureaucracies, technocracies, international corporations. These 'invisible powers' have invaded our everyday life in ways which no amount of parliamentary legislation can check adequately. Bobbio contends that just as the civil rights of freedom of expression and assembly regardless of sex, creed or colour established the framework for parliamentary democracy, so social rights provide the precondition for democratic control of the various aspects of social life.

At first it might seem that Bobbio's proposal does not differ substantially from the calls of other theorists for more democracy, and must suffer from similar drawbacks to theirs. However, Bobbio does address the two main objections we noted about these schemes. First, we disputed the claim that increased political participation led to greater social awareness. Bobbio tackles this difficulty by appealing to a Rawlsian-style social contract to create an agreed framework for how politics should be conducted. The 'rule of law' derived from the concept of justice, provides a shared political culture and the juridical foundation for political pluralism. The second, related, problem for direct democracy was its inefficiency in turning preferences into policies, and the potential ignoring of relevant opinions or intense minorities as a result. Bobbio seeks to rectify this problem by maintaining political parties as the medium for increasing the democratization of society. He argues that they provide the best basis for providing voters with political choices and representing their diverse interests. Thus although political debate occurs within a single system of beliefs about how democratic politics should be conducted and what our social rights and obligations are, these commitments facilitate rather than inhibit the expression of a plurality of political views. For it adds up to a shared conceptual and institutional framework for the effective competition between differing individuals about how society should be run.

To recapitulate, Bobbio seeks to adapt the foundations and institutions of liberal democracy to meet the demands and criticisms of socialists. He fully accepts the left's contention that the inequalities of wealth and influence, the growth of bureaucratic and corporative organizations and the increasing complexity, sophistication and specialization of modern societies have undermined the democratic accountability of governments and empowered other agencies that have never been subject to public scrutiny. The Marxist solution of simply identifying the individual's interest with those of the community has long been discredited, and Bobbio aligns himself with a prominent tradition of Italian socialist thought in rejecting it. Instead he suggests a reform of liberal justifications for civil and political equality to include social equality as the natural extension and partner of the other two. Following Rawls, he proposes a new social contract as the basis of a democratic society which places our social and political rights and duties on an uncompromising individualist ethical foundation. He complements this socialist reformulation of liberal theory with a number of proposals for restructuring the institutional framework of liberalism. He argues that we need to render not only the state but society democratically accountable. However, in order to avoid the counter-productive inflation of political activity and the particularist tendencies of traditional radical calls for participatory democracy, he maintains that a multi-party system operating within a strong legal framework guaranteeing citizen's rights provides the most practicable avenue for reform.

Bobbio's analysis and proposals will undoubtedly be the object of debate and criticism, particularly from the left. Yet if socialists wish to make their enthusiasm for 'freedom and fairness' more than a party political slogan they need to rethink drastically the relationship between state and society under socialism. As Bobbio shows, this involves not only the democratization of society, but the socialization of democracy as well. Bobbio's book is to be welcomed, therefore, as a spur to that reappraisal and the detailed working-out of what, in practical as well as theoretical terms, 'democratic socialism' means.

Richard Bellamy
Jesus College, Cambridge.

# Preface

This slim volume brings together some of my recent articles on the so-called 'transformations' of democracy. I use the term 'transformation' in an essentially neutral sense, without positive or negative connotations. I prefer to talk of transformation rather than of crisis, because 'crisis' suggests an imminent collapse. Democracy is not enjoying the best of health in the world today, and indeed has never enjoyed it in the past, but nor does it have one foot in the grave. Whatever is said about it, the fact remains that none of the democratic regimes which came into being after the Second World War have been destroyed by a dictatorship, as happened after the First World War. Quite the reverse: some dictatorships which survived the catastrophe of the war have been changed into democracies. While the Soviet world is periodically shaken by democratic tremors, the world of Western democracies is not seriously threatened by fascist movements.

For a democratic system, the process of 'becoming', of transformation, is its natural state. Democracy is dynamic, despotism is static and always essentially the same. Democratic theorists at the end of the eighteenth century contrasted modern democracy (representative) with the democracy of the ancients (direct). But they would have had no hesitation in considering the despotism of their day the equivalent of that first described by classical writers: one only has to think of the category of oriental despotism used by Montesquieu and Hegel. There have also been those who, rightly or wrongly, have applied the concept of oriental despotism to explain the existing state in the Soviet Union. When we talk of Western democracies today we are referring to regimes which emerged within the last two hundred years, after the American and French Revolutions. Even so, C. B. Macpherson has believed it possible to identify at least four phases in the development of modern democracy between its origins in the eighteenth century and today.

I have selected those essays from among my writings which, without relating to specific events, seemed to me to have a certain topicality. The opening article, which provides the title of the collection, was written last. It originated as a lecture given in November 1983 to the Spanish Parliament at the invitation of its president, Professor Gregorio Peces-Barba. I then revised and developed it further, presenting it as the introductory paper to the international conference 'The Future Has Already Begun' organized by Professor Francesco Barone and held in May 1984 at Locarno. It represents a summary of the transformations of democracy in terms of 'broken promises', that is, in terms of the gap between the ideal of democracy as it was conceived by its founding fathers and the reality of democracy as we have come to experience it, with varying degrees of participation, on a day to day basis.

After the Locarno debate I feel I should specify more clearly that, among the broken promises – namely the survival of invisible power, the persistence of oligarchies, the suppression of mediating bodies, the renewed vigour in the representation of particular interests, the break-down of participation, the failure to educate citizens (or to educate them properly) – some could not objectively be kept and were thus illusions from the outset, others were not so much promises as misplaced hopes, still others as it turned out came up against unforeseen obstacles. In none of these circumstances is it appropriate to speak of the 'degeneration' of democracy. It is better instead to speak in terms of the natural consequences of adapting abstract principles to reality, or of the inevitable contamination of theory when it is forced to submit to the demands of practice. This applies to all the broken promises but one: the presence (and robust constitution) of invisible power which, in a country like Italy, survives alongside visible power. Democracy is open to the most conflicting definitions, but there is none which can fail to include as one of its defining characteristics: the 'visibility' or transparency of power. Elias Cannetti has written: 'The secret resides within the innermost nucleus of power.' The creators of the first democratic regimes set themselves the task of bringing into being a form of government in which this hard nucleus would be destroyed once and for all (see chapter 4, *Democracy and Invisible Power*). There is no doubt that the continued existence of oligarchies or of elites in power is incompatible with democratic ideals. The fact remains that there is still a substantial difference between a political system in which several elites are in direct competition in the electoral arena, and a system where there exists a single power group which renews itself through co-opting fresh members. While the presence of an invisible power corrupts democracy, the existence of power groups which take it in turns to govern via free elections remains, at least to this day, the only concrete form in which democratic principles have been realized. Something similar is occurring now that attempts are being made to extend democratic procedures to centres of power which traditionally have been autocratic, such as big business or bureaucracy. The fact that there are limits to what can be achieved is less a question of failure than of stunted development. As for the representation of vested interests which is gradually eroding the sphere which should have been reserved exclusively for political representation, this, like it or not, is none other than a form of alternative democracy, which has natural room to develop in a capitalist society where the real protagonists of political action are increasingly organized groups, and hence is a system very different from the one envisaged by democratic theory, which was not inclined to recognize that any intermediary entity existed between individual citizens and the nation as a whole. If what we mean by crisis is the growing influence of interest groups, and the con-comitant phenomenon of decisions being increasingly taken via agreements between the various parties involved, what is at issue is not so much democracy as the traditional image of the sovereign state placed above particular interests (see chapter 6, *Contract and Contractarianism in the Current Debate*). Finally there is the failure to use education to instill effectively the principles of citizenship so as to enable the citizens, once they are entrusted with the right to choose who governs them, to vote for the wisest, the most honest, the most enlightened of their fellow citizens. This however should be considered not so much a broken promise, as an excessively benevolent conception of human beings as political animals: they pursue their own interests in the political sphere just as much as they do in the economic sphere. But no one nowadays thinks that it is a refutation of democracy to maintain, as has been argued for years, that the vote is a piece of merchandise which is acquired by whoever makes the best offer.

Of course all this line of argument only holds as long as we keep to what I have called the minimal definition of democracy. According to this a 'democratic regime' is taken to mean first and foremost a set of procedural rules for arriving at collective decisions in a way which accommodates and facilitates the fullest possible participation of interested parties. I fully realize that such a procedural or formal (or, in a pejorative sense, formalistic) definition seems inadequate in the eyes of movements which claim to be left wing. But, apart from the fact that no other definition exists which is as clear, this is the only one offering an infallible criterion which allows a major distinction to be made from the outset between two opposed ideal-types of government, independently of any value judgement. Indeed, it is worth adding straight away that if we include in the general concept of democracy the strategy of reaching a compromise between different parties through free debate so as to arrive at a majority decision, the definition proposed here corresponds to the reality of representative democracy (irrespective of whether we are dealing with political representation or with interest groups) better than to the reality of direct democracy. The referendum, being confined to framing questions only in the form of 'either/or', militates against compromise and favours conflict, and for precisely this reason is more suited for settling issues of principle than for resolving conflicts of interest (see chapter 2, *Representative and Direct Democracy*). It is also appropriate to specify at this point, especially to those who place renewed hope in the transformation of society through the birth of new political movements, that while democracy as a method is indeed open to all possibilities, it is equally adamant in demanding that its institutions be respected, because all its advantages as a method hinge on this respect, and among these institutions it is the political parties alone which are authorized to act as intermediaries between individuals and government (see chapter 3, *The Constraints of Democracy*).

I do not rule out the possibility that this insistence on the rules, that is to say on formal rather than substantive considerations, may be the result of the professional idiosyncracy, or *déformation professionelle*, of someone who has been teaching for decades in a faculty of law. But a democratic regime can only function properly within the limits of the type of government which, according to a tradition going back to classical times, is called 'the rule of law' (see chapter 3, *The Rule of Men or the Rule of Law*). I am referring to an idea I formulated some time ago, namely that law and power are two sides of the same coin: only power can create law and only law can limit power. The despotic state is the ideal-type of a state considered from the point of view of power; at the other extreme there is the democratic state which is the ideal-type of state considered from the point of view of law. When classical thinkers extolled the rule of law and contrasted it with the rule of men, they had in mind laws derived from tradition or laid down by great legislators. Nowadays when we talk of the rule of law we are thinking primarily of the basic laws of the constitution, which establish not so much what those in government should do as how laws should be passed. These are laws which are binding on the government even more so than on ordinary citizens: by this we mean the rule of law at a higher level, and one where the legislators themselves are subject to binding principles. An arrangement of this kind is possible only if those who exercise power at all levels are in the last resort accountable to the original holders of ultimate power, the individual members of the public.

It can never be stressed enough in the face of the permanent temptation exerted by organic theories of society (something not entirely unknown in left-wing political thought) that democratic theory is based on an individualistic conception of society. This it shares with liberalism (see chapter 5, *Liberalism Old and New*); and this explains why modern democracy has made advances in the past, and now only exists, wherever the basic freedoms have been constitutionally recognized. It goes without saying that no individualist conception of society, whether ontological or methodological, discounts the fact that human beings are social animals who cannot and do not live in isolation. But the relationship between the individual and society is seen by liberalism and democracy in different ways: liberalism severs the organic bonds which connect individuals with the community and make thim live, at least for most of their lives, outside their mother's womb, plunging them into an unknown world full of dangers in which they have to struggle to survive. Democracy creates new bonds between the individual and their fellow human beings, because their artificial union allows society to be reconstituted not as an organic whole but as an association of free individuals. The former stresses the capacity of individuals self-development; the latter extols above all their ability to overcome isolation through a number of shrewd devices which have at last made possible the institution of a political system which is not tyrannical. It comes down to two different ways of conceiving individual potential: either as a microcosm, as a self-contained whole, or alternatively as an entity which is indivisible but can combine with other similar entities in various ways to form a larger entity at a higher level.

All the essays brought together here deal with very general problems and are (or rather set out to be) elementary. They have been written for the reading public who are interested in politics and not for the specialist. They are essays which once would have been classified as 'popular philosophy'. They were prompted by one central consideration: to bring democracy down to earth, from the realm of ethereal principles to where there are flesh-and-blood interests in conflict. I have always considered this to be the only way to come to terms with the contradictions which assail a democratic society and with the tortuous route it must follow to resolve rather than succumb to them. In this way it is possible to acknowledge democracy's endemic vices without losing heart and without giving up any faint hope of improving it. If I were to imagine the type of adversary whom I would like, not perhaps to convince, but make less suspicious of democracy, it is not those critics who spurn it as the government of the incompetent, i.e. the perennial extreme Right which continually re-emerges in the most varied guises but always harbours the same grudge against the 'immortal principles' of 1789. The ones I have in mind are those who, seeing this democracy of ours, always fragile, always vulnerable, corruptible and frequently corrupt, would seek to destroy it in order to render it perfect; those who, to use the famous image of Hobbes, behave like the daughters of Pelia who hacked their old father to pieces so that he would be born again. To start a dialogue with the first type of reader is liable to be a waste of time. To continue one with the second enables us not to lose hope in the power of common sense.

# 1

# The Future of Democracy

AN UNINVITED PREFACE

I have been invited to give a paper on the future of democracy, a subject more fraught with pitfalls than most, and I will cover myself at the outset with two quotations. In his lectures on the philosophy of history at Berlin University, Hegel, faced with a question put to him by a student about whether the United States should be considered the country of the future, replied, patently irritated: 'As a country of the future, America is of no interest to us here, for prophecy is not the business of the philosopher . . . In philosophy we are concerned with that which *is*, both now and eternally – in short with reason. And that is quite enough to occupy our attention.'[1] In his famous lecture on science as a vocation delivered to students of Munich University at the end of the First World War, Max Weber replied as follows to members of the audience who insisted on asking what his opinion was on the future of Germany: 'The prophet and the demagogue do not belong on the academic platform'.[2]

Even someone who is not inclined to accept the lines of reasoning adopted by Hegel and Weber and who considers them a lame excuse must surely acknowledge that the job of the prophet is a hazardous one. The difficulty of knowing the future also derives from the fact that all of us project our own aspirations and anxieties into it, while history follows its course blithely indifferent to our concerns, a course shaped by millions and millions of little, minute, human acts which no intellect, however powerful, has ever been capable of synthesizing into a synoptic view which is not too abstract to be credible. For this reason the forecasts made by the masters of thought on the course of the world have in the event turned out to be almost always wrong, not least the predictions of the person whom a section of humanity believed and still believes to be the founder of a new and infallible science of society: Karl Marx.

Briefly my opinion is the following: if you ask me whether democracy has a future and, assuming it has one, what it will be, I have no qualms in replying that I do not know. The object of this paper is purely and simply to make some observations on the current state of democratic regimes, and, to echo Hegel, we have our work cut out doing this. If, on the basis of these observations, it were then possible to extrapolate a trend with regard to the progress (or regress) of these regimes, and thus to attempt a cautious prognosis of their future, so much the better.

## A MINIMAL DEFINITION OF DEMOCRACY

My premiss is that the only way a meaningful discussion of democracy, as distinct from all forms of autocratic government, is possible is to consider it as characterized by a set of rules (primary or basic) which establish *who* is authorised to take collective decisions and which *procedures* are to be applied. Every social group needs to take decisions binding on all members of the group so as to ensure its own survival, both internally and externally.[3] But even group decisions are made by individuals (the group as such does not decide anything). As a result, for a decision, taken by individuals (one, several, many, all together) to be accepted as a collective decision, it is necessary for it to be taken on the basis of rules (whether written or customary) which lay down who are the individuals authorized to take the decisions binding on all the members of the group and what procedures are to be used. As for the persons called upon to take (or collaborate in the taking of) collective decisions, a democracy is characterized by conferring this power (which, in so far as it is authorized by the basic law of the constitution, becomes a right) to a large number of members of the group. I realize the phrase 'a large number' is vague. But, apart from the fact that political pronouncements issue forth from the realm of the 'nearly' and 'mostly', it is wrong to say all, because even in the most perfect democratic system, individuals cannot vote until they have reached a certain age. 'Omnicracy', or the rule of everyone, is an ideal upper limit. What number of individuals must have the vote before it is possible to start talking of a democracy cannot be established in terms of an abstract principle, i.e. leaving out of account historical circumstances and the need for a yardstick to make any judgement. All that can be said is that a society in which the ones to have the vote are adult male citizens is more democratic than one in which only property owners have the vote, and less democratic than one in which women also have the vote. The statement that in the last century there occurred in some countries a continuous process of democratization means that the number of those entitled to vote steadily increased.

As for the mode in which decisions are arrived at, the basic rule of democracy is the rule of the majority, in other words the rule according to which decisions are considered collective, and thus binding on the whole group, if they are approved by at least the majority of those entrusted with taking the decision. If a majority decision is valid, a unanimous decision is all the more valid.[4] But unanimity is possible only in a limited or homogenous group and can be demanded only in two extreme and diametrically opposed cases: either when a very serious decision is involved, so that everyone taking part has the right of veto; or when the decision has negligible implications, so that someone who does not expressly disagree acquiesces (the case of tacit consent). Naturally unanimity is required when only two people are to decide. This provides a clear distinction between a decision based on genuine agreement and one taken according to the law (which usually involves only majority approval).

Moreover, even a minimal definition of democracy, like the one I adopt, requires more than just conferring the right to participate directly or indirectly in the making of collective decisions on a substantial number of citizens, and more than the existence of procedural rules like majority rule (or in extreme cases unanimity). There is a third condition involved, namely that those called upon to take decisions, or to elect those who are to take decisions, must be offered real alternatives and be in a position to choose between these alternatives. For this condition to be realized those called upon to take decisions must be guaranteed the so-called basic rights: freedom of opinion, of expression, of speech, of assembly, of association etc. These are the rights on which the liberal state has been founded since its inception, giving rise to the doctrine of the *Rechtsstaat*, or juridical state, in the full sense of the term, i.e. the state which not only exercises power *sub lege*, but exercises it within limits derived from the constitutional recognition of the so-called 'inviolable' rights of the individual. Whatever may be the philosophical basis of these rights, they are the necessary precondition for the mainly procedural mechanisms, which characterize a democratic system, to work properly. The constitutional norms which confer these rights are not rules of the game as such: they are preliminary rules which allow the game to take place.

From this it follows that the liberal state is not only the historical but the legal premiss of the democratic state. The liberal state and the democratic state are doubly interdependent: if liberalism provides those liberties necessary for the proper exercise of democratic power, democracy guarantees the existence and persistence of fundamental liberties. In other words: an illiberal state is unlikely to ensure the proper workings of democracy, and conversely an undemocratic state is unlikely to be able to safeguard basic liberties. The historical proof of this interdependence is provided by the fact that when both liberal and democratic states fall they fall together.

IDEALS AND BRUTE FACTS

Having outlined the basic principles I am now in a position to get down to the subject at issue and offer some observations on the present state of democracy. We are dealing with a topic which is usually debated under the heading 'the transformations of democracy'. A collection of everything that has been written about the transformations of democracy would fill a library. But the word 'transformation' is so vague that it allows radically different assessments. For the Right (I have in mind for example the book *The Transformation of Democracy*[5] by V. Pareto, founding father of a long and continuous tradition of laments about the crisis of civilization), democracy has been transformed into a semi-anarchic regime which will bring about the 'disintegration' of the state. For the Left (I am thinking of a book like the one by J. Agnoli, *Die Transformation der Demokratie*,[6] typical of 'extra-parliamentary' criticism), parliamentary democracy is progressively turning into an autocratic regime. Rather than concentrate on the notion of transformation, I believe it is more useful for our purposes to reflect on the gap between democratic ideals and 'actually existing democracy' (an expression I am using in the same sense as when people talk of 'actually existing socialism'). Someone in a lecture once drew my attention to the concluding words which Pasternak puts in the mouth of Gordon, the friend of doctor Zhivago. 'This has happened several times in the course of history. A thing which has been conceived in a lofty, ideal manner is transformed into brute facts. Thus Rome came out of Greece and the Russian Revolution came out of the Russian Enlightenment.'[7] In a similar way, I will add, the liberal and democratic thought of Locke, Rousseau, Tocqueville, Bentham or John Stuart Mill turned into the actions of ... (you can fill in yourselves any name you see fit – you will easily be able to find more than one). It is precisely these 'brute facts' and not what has been conceived as 'noble and lofty ideals' which are at issue here; or, put another way, what is at issue here is the contrast between what was promised and what has actually come about. I will single out six of these broken promises.

## THE BIRTH OF THE PLURALIST SOCIETY

Democracy was born of an individualistic conception of society, at variance with the organic conception which prevailed in classical times and in the intervening period and according to which the whole has primacy over its parts. Instead it conceives every form of society, especially political society, as an artificial product formed by the will of individuals. The emergence of the individualistic conception of society and the state and the decline of the organic conception can be accounted for by the interaction of three events in the history of ideas which are characteristic of social philosophy in the modern age.

(1) The contractarian theories of the seventeenth and eighteenth centuries whose initial hypothesis that civil society is preceded by a state of nature in which sovereign power is exercised by free and equal individuals who agree among themselves to bring into existence a communal power entrusted with the function of guaranteeing their life and liberty (as well as their property).

(2) The birth of political economy, that is to say of an analysis of society and of social relations whose subject is once again the individual human being, *homo oeconomicus,* not the *politikon zoon* of traditional thought, who is considered not in his own right but as the member of a community. This individual, according to Adam Smith, 'in pursuing his own interest, often promotes the interests of society more effectively than if he set out to actually promote them'. (Indeed, according to Macpherson's interpretation, the state of nature conceived by Hobbes and Locke is a prefiguration of a market society).[8]

(3) The utilitarian philosophy of Bentham and Mill, for which only one criterion can serve as the basis of an objective ethical system, and hence distinguish good from evil, without resorting to vague concepts such as 'nature' and the like. This criterion takes as its starting point the consideration of essentially personal states of mind, such as pleasure and pain, and thus resolves the traditional problem of the common good by defining it as the sum of individual good, or, in Bentham's formula, as the happiness of the greatest number.

By adopting the hypothesis of the sovereignty of the individual, who, by reaching agreement with other individuals who are equally sovereign, creates political society, democratic doctrine imagined a state without the intermediary bodies which characterize the corporatist society of medieval cities, or the state composed of various ranks and estates which necessarily preceded the institution of absolute monarchies. It envisaged a political society without any subsidiary associations of particular interests intervening between the sovereign people made up of so many individuals (one man one vote) and its representatives. There would be none of the factions so hated by Rousseau, and deprived of legal influence by the law of Le Chapelier (rescinded in France as late as 1887). What has actually happened in democratic states is the exact opposite: increasingly it is less and less the individual who is the most influential factor in politics and more and more it is the group: large organizations, associations of all kinds, trade unions of every conceivable profession, political parties of widely differing ideologies. Groups and not individuals are the protagonists of political life in a democratic society: there is no longer one sovereign power, namely the people or nation, composed of individuals who have acquired the right to participate directly or indirectly in government, the people conceived as an ideal (or mystical) unit. Instead the people are divided into opposing and conflicting groups, all relatively autonomous in relation to central government (an autonomy which individual human beings have lost or have never had, except in an ideal model of government which has always been refuted by the facts).

The ideal model of democratic society was a centripetal society. The reality is a centrifugal society, which has not just one centre of power (the 'general will' envisaged by Rousseau), but a plethora of them, and which deserves the name, as political scientists agree, of polycentric society or polyarchy (or, put more strongly but not altogether incorrectly, a 'polycracy'). The model of the democratic state, based on popular sovereignty, was conceived in the image of, and as analogous to, the sovereignty of the prince, and hence was a monist model of society. The real society underlying democratic government is pluralist.

### THE RENEWED VIGOUR OF PARTICULAR INTERESTS

This primary transformation of democracy (primary in the sense that it concerns the distribution of power) gives rise to the second which concerns the nature of representation. Modern democracy, which came into being as representative democracy, was meant, in contrast to the democracy of classical times, to be epitomized by a system of political representation, i.e. a form of representation in which the representative who is called on to pursue the interests of the nation cannot be subject to a binding mandate. The principle on which political representation is based is the exact antithesis of the one underlying the representation of particular interests, where the representative, having to support the cause of the person represented, is subject to a binding mandate (a feature of private law which makes provisions for the contract being revoked in cases where the mandate has been exceeded). One of the most famous and historically significant debates held in the French Constituent Assembly, which gave birth to the Constitution of 1791, witnessed the victory of those who maintained that the deputy, once elected, became the representative of the nation and no longer of the electorate: as such he was no longer bound by any mandate. The unrestricted mandate had previously been a prerogative of the king who, on convening the *états généraux*, had claimed that the delegates of the estates had not been sent to the assembly with *pouvoirs restrictifs*.[9] As an overt expression of sovereignty, unrestricted mandate was transferred from the sovereignty of the king to the sovereignty of the assembly elected by the people. Ever since then, the veto on binding mandates has become an axiomatic rule in all constitutions based on democratic representation, and where democracy has had to fight for survival it has always found convinced supporters in those who defended representative democracy against attempts to replace it by, or integrate it with, representation of particular interests.

No constitutional norm has ever been more violated than the veto on binding mandates. No principle has been more disregarded than that of political representation. But in a society composed of relatively autonomous groups competing to gain supremacy, to assert their own interests over those of other groups, could such a norm, such a principle, ever be realized in practice? Apart from the fact that every group tends to identify the national interest with its own, is there any general criterion which would enable us to distinguish the common interest from the particular interest of this or that group, or from the combination of particular interests of groups which come to an arrangement among themselves at the expense of others? Whoever represents particular interests always has a binding mandate. And where can we find a representative who does not represent particular interests? Certainly not in trade unions, for the drawing up of wage agreements depends on them as do national agreements concerning the organization and cost of labour, all of which have an enormous political impact. In parliament? But what does party discipline signify if not an open violation of the veto on restricted mandates? Every now and then some deputies take advantage of the secret ballot to give party discipline the slip, but are they not branded in Italy as 'snipers', that is as renegades to be singled out for public disapproval? The veto on restricted mandates, when all is said and done, is a rule without any sanctions attached. On the contrary, the only sanction feared by the deputy, whose re-election depends on the continued support of his party, is the one applied if he transgresses the opposite principle of toeing the official line, thus obliging him to consider himself bound by the mandate given to him by his party.

Confirmation of the victory – I would dare to say a definitive one – of the representation of interests over impartial political representation is provided by the type of relationship, which is coming to be the norm in most democratic states in Europe, between opposed interest groups (representatives of industrialists and workers respectively) and parliament. This relationship has brought about a new type of social system which is called, rightly or wrongly, 'neo-corporatism',[10] and is characterized by a triangular arrangement in which the government, ideally the representative of national interests, intervenes only as a mediator between the two sides and at most can act as guarantor (generally an impotent one) to ensure that any agreement reached is honoured. Those who some ten years ago thought out this model, which is now at the centre of the debate on the 'transformations' of democracy, defined a neo-corporatist society as offering a solution to social conflicts involving a procedure, that of agreement between large organizations, which has nothing to do with political representation but instead is the typical expression of the representation of particular interests.

### THE SURVIVAL OF OLIGARCHIES

The third unfulfilled promise of democracy concerns its failure to put an end to oligarchical power. I have no need to dwell on this point because the subject has been extensively dealt with and is uncontroversial, at least since the end of the last century when Gaetano Mosca propounded his theory of the political class which, due to Pareto's influence, came to be known as the theory of elites.[11] The guiding principle of democratic thought has always been liberty, understood in the sense of autonomy, that is, the ability to be governed by one's own laws (according to Rousseau's famous definition). This should lead to the perfect identification between the person who lays down a rule of conduct and the one who submits to it, and hence to the elimination of the traditional distinction, which is the basis of all political thinking, between the governed and those who govern. Representative democracy, which is after all the only form of democracy which actually exists and is operative, is by its very nature a renunciation of the principle of liberty as autonomy. The hypothesis that the future 'computer-ocracy', as it has been called, might make direct democracy possible, by giving all citizens the possibilty of transmitting their votes to an electronic brain, is puerile. To judge by the number of laws which are tabled every year in Italy, responsible citizens would have to be called upon to cast their vote at least once a day. Such an excess of participation, which produces the phenomenon which Dahrendorf has pejoratively called that of the 'total citizen', only results in the political satiety and increasing apathy of the electorate.[12] The price which has to be paid for the commitment of the few is often the indifference of the many. Nothing risks killing off democracy more effectively than an excess of democracy.

Naturally the fact that elites are present in the power structure does not eliminate the difference between democratic and autocratic regimes. Even Mosca realized this, though he was a conservative who professed to be a liberal but not a democrat, and who worked out a complex typology of forms of government with a view to demonstrating that, while oligarchies will always be found in power, distinctions can be made between different forms of government on the basis of the different ways they are formed and organized. As my starting point was a largely procedural definition of democracy, it should not be forgotten that one of the advocates of this interpretation, Joseph Schumpeter, struck the nail on the head when he argued that the defining characteristic of a democratic regime is not the absence of elites but the presence of several elites in competition with each other for the votes of the public. In C. B. Macpherson's book, *The Life and Times of Liberal Democracy*,[13] four phases are identified in the development of democracy from the last century to the present: the current phase, which he defines as 'democracy of equilibrium', corresponds to Schumpeter's definition. An Italian elitist who is an expert on Mosca and Pareto, made a concise but, in my view, telling distinction between elites which *impose* themselves and elites which *propose* themselves.[14]

## LIMITED SPACE

If democracy has been unsuccessful in completely defeating oligarchical power, it has been even less successful in penetrating all the spaces in which the power to make decisions binding on an entire social group is exercised. In this context the relevant distinction is no longer between the power of the few and of the many, but between ascending and descending power. Moreover, it is more appropriate in this matter to speak of inconsistency than of broken promises, since modern democracy came into being as a method for legitimizing and regulating political decisions in the strict sense of the term, or of the 'government' as such, whether national or local, where individuals are taken into account in their general role as citizens, and not in their many particular roles as members of a religious faith, as workers, as soldiers, as consumers, as invalids etc. Once universal suffrage has been achieved, if it is possible to speak of the process of democratization being extended this should manifest itself less in the transition from representative to direct democracy, as is often maintained, than in the transition from political to social democracy. The issue is less a question of 'who votes?' than of 'where does one vote?.' In other words, when people want to know if a development towards greater democracy has taken place in a certain country, what should be looked for is an increase, not in the number of those who have the right to participate in making the decisions which concern them, but in the number of contexts or spaces in which they can exercise this right. As long as the process of democratization has not made inroads into the two great blocks of power from above which exist in developed societies, big business and bureaucracy – leaving aside whether this would be desirable even if it were possible – the process of democratization cannot be said to be complete.

However I am intrigued to observe that in those spaces which are, in traditional terms, non-political, for example in the factory, there has been a declaration of certain liberties within that specific power system analogous to the declaration of the rights of the citizen *vis à vis* the political power system. I am thinking of, for example, the Italian Workers' Statute of 1970, and of the current efforts to draw up a charter of patients' rights. Even where the prerogatives of the citizen *vis à vis* the state are concerned, the concession of the right to certain liberties preceded the granting of political rights. As I said when talking about the relationship of the liberal state to the democratic state, the concession of political rights has been a natural consequence of the concession of basic liberties; the only guarantee that the right to liberties will be respected consists in the right to control in the last instance the power which underwrites this guarantee.

## INVISIBLE POWER

The fifth promise unfulfilled by the reality of democracy when compared to the ideal is the elimination of invisible power.[15] While the literature on the relationship between democracy and oligarchical power is immense, the subject of invisible power has so far remained largely neglected (partly because it cannot be researched using the techniques usually employed by sociologists, such as interviews, opinion polls etc.). It may be that I am particularly influenced by what happens in Italy, where the presence of invisible power (mafia, camorra, anomalous Masonic lodges, secret services which are a law unto themselves, authorities who ought to be keeping a check on subversive elements but instead are protecting them) is, if you pardon the play on words, highly conspicuous. The fact remains, however, that the most extensive research on this subject I have come across so far is a book by an American scholar, Alan Wolfe, *The Limits of Legitimacy*,[16] which dedicates a well-documented chapter to what he calls the 'double state', double in the sense that according to him there exists an invisible state alongside the visible state. It is well known that democracy, when it first appeared, held out the prospect of ridding human society for ever of invisible power, so as to give birth to a form of government which would have carried on its business in public, 'au grand jour' (as Maurice Joly put it).[17] Modern democracy made the democracy of the Ancient World as its model, and in particular the halcyon days of the tiny city of Athens, when the people assembled in the *agora* and freely took their decisions in the clear light of day, having heard the orators illustrating the various points of view. Plato denigrated it (but Plato was anti-democratic) by calling it 'theatrocracy' (a word found, significantly enough, in Nietzsche). One of the reasons for the superiority of democracy over the absolute states which had reasserted the value of *arcana imperii*, the secrets of authority, and defended with historical and political arguments the need for major political decisions to be made in secret cabinet-meetings, far from the indiscreet gaze of the public, was based on the conviction that democratic government could finally bring about the transparency of power, 'power without masks'.

In the Appendix to *Perpetual Peace* Kant formulated and illustrated the basic principle according to which 'All actions relating to the rights of other men are wrong, if the maxims from which they follow are inconsistent with publicity.'[18] This means that an action which I am forced to keep secret is certainly an action not only unjust, but one which if it were made public would provoke such a strong reaction that carrying it out would be impossible. Which state, to give the example Kant uses himself, could declare publicly, in the actual moment of signing an international treaty, that it will not honour it? Which civil servant can declare in public that he will use public money for private purposes? What results from framing the problem in these terms is that the principle that all acts of government must be open to public scrutiny is important not only, as is usually said, to permit the citizen to be aware of the acts of those in power and hence control them, but also because public scrutiny is itself a form of control, is a device which allows distinctions to be made between what is permissible and what is not. It is no coincidence that politics based on the *arcana imperii* went hand in hand with theories of *raison d'état*, i.e. with theories according to which the state is permitted what is denied to private citizens and thus the state is forced to act in secret so as not to cause an outrage. (To give some idea of the exceptional power of the tyrant, Plato says that only the tyrant is allowed to perform in public scandalous acts which ordinary mortals imagine performing only in their dreams).[17] Needless to say public accountability of power is all the more necessary in a state like ours, in which technological progress has increasingly given the authorities a practically unlimited power to monitor everything citizens are doing, down to the last detail. If I earlier expressed reservations about whether the 'computer-ocracy' is of benefit to those governed in a democracy, I have no doubt about the service it can perform to those who govern. The ideal of the powerful has always been to see every gesture and to listen to every word of their subjects (if possible without being seen or heard): nowadays this ideal is realizable. No despot in antiquity, no absolute monarch of the modern age, even if surrounded by a thousand informers, has ever succeeded in having all the information on his subjects that the most democratic governments can obtain using electronic brains. The old question running through the history of political thought: 'Who guards the guards?', can now be reformulated as 'Who controls the controllers?' If no adequate answer can be found to this question, democracy, in the sense of visible government, is lost. In this case we are dealing not so much with a broken promise but with a trend which actually contradicts the basic premisses of democracy, a trend not towards the greatest possible control of those in power by the citizens, but towards the greatest control of the subjects by those in power.

## THE UNEDUCATED CITIZEN

The sixth broken promise concerns the education of the citizen. All the apologias made on behalf of democracy over the last two centuries have included the argument that the only way of making a citizen out of a subject is to confer on him or her those rights which writers on public law in the nineteenth century termed *activae civitatis*. Education for democracy takes place as an integral part of the operation of democracy in practice. It is not a precondition of it: it was not conceived as a precondition even in the Jacobin model, according to which the revolutionary dictatorship comes first and only subsequently the reign of virtue. No, for the good democrat the reign of virtue (which for Montesquieu constituted the basic principle of democracy as opposed to fear, the basis of despotism) is equated with democracy, which not only cannot do without virtue, understood in terms of love of the *res publica*, but at the same time promotes it, feeds it and reinforces it.

One of the classic expressions of this notion can be found in the chapter on ideal government in John Stuart Mill's *Considerations on Representative Government*. He distinguishes active from passive citizens, and specifies that while, in general, rulers prefer the latter, because it is so much easier to keep docile or apathetic subjects in their place, democracy needs the former. He deduces from this that if passive citizens were to predominate rulers would gladly turn their subjects into a flock of sheep, interested only in grazing next to each other (and who are not to complain, I might add, even when there are meagre supplies of grass).[20] This led him to propose the enlargement of suffrage to include the lower classes, on the principle that one of the remedies to the tyranny of the majority is precisely to involve in elections not only the well-off, who always constitute a minority of the population and tend naturally to serve their own exclusive interests, but the lower classes as well. He said participation in elections has a great educative value; it is via political discussion that the worker transcends his repetitious work within the narrow confines of the factory, and is able to understand the relationship between distant events and his own interests, and have contact with citizens different from those he has dealings with in everyday life and thus consciously become a member of a community.[21] Education for citizenship was one of the favourite subjects (treated under the heading 'political culture') of American political science in the 1950s, and rivers of ink flowed on the subject which rapidly dried and faded. Among the many categories they created I remember the distinction they made between a 'society of subjects', i.e. geared to the outputs of the system, that is to the benefits which the electorate hopes to derive from the political system, and a 'society of participants', i.e. geared to inputs, which is formed by voters who consider themselves potentially involved in articulating demands and formulating decisions.

Taking stock of the present situation, the most well-established democracies are impotent before the phenomenon of increasing political apathy, which has overtaken about half of those with the right to vote. In terms of political culture these are people without any orientation, either to outputs or inputs of the system. They are simply unconcerned by what is being done by bureaucrats at the local town hall, which is neatly called in Italian *il palazzo*, 'the palace'. I am aware that political apathy admits of more benign interpretations. But even the most benign interpretations cannot make me forget that all the great democratic theorists would find it difficult to see the renunciation of the right to vote as the beneficial outcome of education to citizenship. In democratic regimes, like the Italian one, in which the percentage of voters is still very high (but is declining with every election that passes), there are good reasons to believe that the use of the vote as an expression of opinion is declining, while what is increasing is the use of the vote as a means of exchange. Thus in the ascetic terminology of the political scientist, the vote is becoming geared towards outputs; or, to use a cruder but less obscurantist phrase, is being 'bought', a type of *clientelismo* based on the often illusory principle of *do ut des* (political support in exchange for personal favours). But I cannot help thinking of Tocqueville who, in a speech to the Chamber of Deputies (27 January 1848) complained about the degeneration of the tenor of public life which meant that 'commonly held opinions, feelings, ideas are being increasingly replaced by particular interests.' Turning to his colleagues, he wondered 'whether the number of those who vote for reasons of vested interest has not increased and the vote of those who decide on the basis of political opinion has not decreased'; he deplored this tendency as the expression of a 'base and vulgar morality', which produces the principle that 'those who have political rights think of using them solely in their own interest.'[22]

## THE RULE OF THE TECHNICIANS

Broken promises. But were they promises that could ever have been kept? I would say not. Leaving aside the natural gulf which I alluded to at the outset between the lofty nobility of the ideal and the brute facts which its realization have brought about, the project of political democracy was conceived for a society much less complex than the one that exists today. The promises were not kept because of obstacles which had not been foreseen or which cropped up unexpectedly as a result of 'transformations' (in this case I believe the term 'transformations' to be appropriate) in the nature of civil society. I will point out three of them.

First, as societies gradually change from a family economy to a market economy, from a market economy to an economy which is protected, regulated and planned, there is an increase in the number of political problems whose solution requires technical expertise. Technical problems require experts, an expanding team of specialized personnel. This had already been noticed over a century ago by Saint-Simon, who had predicted the substitution of the government of jurists by the government of scientists. With the progress of statistical techniques, which outstrip anything which Saint-Simon could have remotely imagined and which only experts are able to use, the need for the so-called 'rule of the technicians' has increased out of all proportion.

Technocracy and democracy are antithetical: if the expert plays a leading role in industrial society he cannot be considered as just any citizen. The hypothesis which underlies democracy is that all are in a position to make decisions about everything. The technocracy claims, on the contrary, that the only ones called on to make decisions are the few who have the relevant expertise. In the time of absolute states, as I have already said, the common people had to be kept at bay from the *arcana imperii* because they were considered too ignorant. Now the common people are certainly less ignorant. But are not the problems to be resolved, problems like the struggle against inflation, securing full employment, ensuring the fair distribution of incomes, becoming increasingly complicated? Do not these problems, by their very nature, require scientific and technical knowledge which are no less arcane for the man or woman in the street (no matter how well educated)?

## THE GROWTH OF THE BUREAUCRATIC APPARATUS

The second unforeseen obstacle to emerge is the continued increase in the scale of bureaucracy, i.e. of a power apparatus arranged hierarchically from top to bottom, and hence diametrically opposed to the system of democratic power. Assuming that grades of power exist in any society, a political system can be visualized as a pyramid; but whereas in a democratic society power is transmitted from the base upwards, in a bureaucratic society power descends from the top.

The democratic state and the bureaucratic state have historically been much more interconnected than might be thought from contrasting them so starkly. All states which have become more democratic have simultaneously become more bureaucratic, because the process of bureaucratization is to a great extent the consequence of the process of democratization. Proof of this is the fact that today the dismantling of the Welfare State, which had necessitated an unprecedented bureaucratic apparatus, conceals the proposal, if not to dismantle democratic power, then certainly to reduce it to within clearly circumscribed limits. The reasons why democratization should have gone hand in hand with bureaucrat-ization, which is after all something Max Weber clearly envisaged, are generally understood. When those who had the right to vote were just property owners, it was natural that they should ask the public authority to perform a single basic function: the protection of private property. This gave rise both to the doctrine of the limited state, the night-watchman state, or, as it is known now, the minimal state, and to the constitution of the state as an association of property owners for the defence of that natural right which was for Locke precisely the right to property. From the moment the vote was extended to the illiterate it was inevitable that they would ask the state to set up free schools, and so take on board a responsibility unknown to the states of traditional oligarchies and of the first bourgeois oligarchy. When the right to vote was also extended to non-property owners, to the have-nots, to those whose only property was their labour, it resulted in them asking the state for protection from unemployment, and in due course for state insurance schemes against illness and old age, for maternity benefits, for subsidized housing etc. So it was that the Welfare State came about, like it or not, as the response to demands emanating from below, demands which were, in the fullest sense of the word, democratic.

### THE INABILITY TO SATISFY DEMAND

The third obstacle is intimately bound up with the question of the overall ability of a democratic system to 'deliver the goods': a problem that in the last few years has provoked debate over the so-called 'ungovernability' of democracy. In essence the central issue is this: first the liberal state, and then by extension the democratic state, have contributed to the emancipation of civil society from the political system. This process of emancipation has created a situation where civil society has increasingly become an inexhaustible source of demands on government, which in order to carry out its functions properly must make adequate responses. But how can government respond if the demands generated by a free society are increasingly numerous, pressing and onerous? As I have said, the necessary precondition for any democratic government is the guarantee of civil liberties: well, freedom of the press, freedom of assembly and association are all channels via which the citizen can appeal to those in government to ask for advantages, benefits, special terms, a more equal distribution of resources. The quantity and rapid turnover of these demands are such that no political system, however efficient, is able to cope with them. This results in the so-called 'overloading' of government and the necessity for the political system to make drastic choices. But one choice excludes another, and not making certain choices produces dissatisfaction.

It does not stop there. The speed with which demands are made of government by citizens is in marked contrast to the slowness with which the complex procedures of a democratic political system allow the political elite to make adequate decisions. As a result the mechanism for inserting demands into the system and the one for extracting responses are increasingly out of phase, the first working at an ever faster rate while the second slows down more and more. This is precisely the opposite of what happens in an autocratic system, which is capable of controlling demand, having previously stifled the autonomy of civil society, and is in practice quicker to make appropriate decisions since it is freed from the obligation to observe complex decision-making procedures like those peculiar to a parliamentary system. In short, democracy is good at generating demands and bad at satisfying them. Autocracy, on the other hand, is in a position to stifle demands and is better placed to meet them.

## IN SPITE OF EVERYTHING

After all I have said so far someone could be excused for expecting a catastrophic vision of the future of democracy. I offer nothing of the kind. Compared with the inter-war years, which were called *L'ère des tyrannies* in the famous book by Elie Halévy[23], democratic regimes have continually enlarged their territory. Juan Linz's book, *The Breakdown of Democracy*,[24] draws mainly on material to do with the aftermath of the First World War. The contrasting book by Julian Santamaria, *The Transition to Democracy in Southern Europe and Latin America*,[25] concentrates on the events following the Second World War. Once the First World War had finished it only took a few years in Italy, and ten in Germany, for the parliamentary state to be overthrown. After the Second World War, where democracy was restored it has not been overthrown, and in other states authoritarian governments have been overthrown. Even in a country like Italy, where democracy is not the ruling force and works inadequately, it is not seriously at risk, even if I utter these words with a certain trepidation.

Let us be clear on this: I am speaking about internal dangers, dangers which could arise from the extreme Right or extreme Left. In Eastern Europe, where democratic regimes were suffocated at birth or are unable to see the light of day, the reason for this has been and continues to be external. In this analysis I have concentrated on the internal difficulties of democracy and not the external ones, which derive from the way different countries work together in the international system. Well, my conclusion is that the broken promises and the unforeseen obstacles which I have surveyed here are not sufficient to 'transform' a democratic regime into an autocratic one. The essential difference between the first and the second has been preserved. The minimal content of the democratic state has not been impaired: guarantees of the basic liberties, the existence of competing parties, periodic elections with universal suffrage, decisions which are collective or the result of compromise (as in consociational democracies or in the neo-corporatist system) or made on the basis of the majority principle, or in any event as the outcome of open debate between the different factions or allies of a government coalition. Some democracies are more unstable, more vulnerable than others and there are different degrees of approximation to the ideal model, but even one which is far removed from the model can in no way be confused with an autocratic state and even less with a totalitarian one.

I have not referred to external threats, because the subject I am addressing is the future of democracy and not the future of humanity. On the latter, I must confess, I am not inclined to place any bets. Parodying the title of our convention: 'The Future Has Already Begun', someone in humourous vein could wonder 'And what if instead the future had already finished?'

However I think I am able to offer a final observation, even if I admit it is a risky one to make: no war has yet broken out between states established as democratic regimes. This does not mean democratic states have not fought wars, but so far they have never fought them *with each other*.[28] This is, as I have said, a bold assertion, but I challenge someone to refute it. Could Kant have been right when he proclaimed that the first definitive clause in a hypothetical treaty to ensure perpetual peace should read 'The constitution of every state should be republican?'[27] Certainly the concept of 'republic' Kant refers to does not coincide with the present concept of 'democracy', but the notion that a safeguard against war would be the internal constitution of states has proved to be the powerful, fertile, inspiring idea behind the many pacifist projects which have succeeded one another over the last two centuries, even if in practice they remained stillborn. The objections raised against Kant's principle have always stemmed from a failure to understand that since it involves a universal principle it holds only if *all*, and not just a few or several, adopt the form of government required to achieve perpetual peace.

### THE APPEAL TO VALUES

To conclude, an answer must be given to the fundamental question, the one I have heard repeated often, especially by the young, so vulnerable to illusions and disappointments. If democracy is mainly a set of procedural rules, how can it claim to rely on 'active citizens'? To have active citizens are not perhaps ideals necessary? Of course ideals are necessary. But how can anyone ignore the great struggles over ideals which have produced these rules? Shall we try to enumerate them?

First and foremost, the ideal of toleration emerges only after centuries of cruel wars of religion. If today there is a threat to world peace this is once again due to fanaticism, in other words to blind belief in having a monopoly of truth and having the requisite force to impose it on others. It is useless to cite examples: they are right in front of our eyes every day. Second, there is the ideal of non-violence: I have never forgotten Karl Popper's dictum according to which the essential distinction between a democratic state and a non-democratic one is that only in the former can citizens get rid of their government without bloodshed.[26] The formal rules of democracy, which are so frequently derided, have introduced for the first time into history techniques for coexistence designed to resolve social conflict without recourse to violence. Only where these rules are respected is the adversary no longer an enemy (to be destroyed), but an opponent who tomorrow may be in our shoes. Third, there is the ideal of the gradual renewal of society via the free debate of ideas and the modification of attitudes and ways of life: only democracy allows silent revolutions to take shape and spread, as has happened in the case of the relationship between the sexes in the last few decades, which is probably the greatest revolution of our age. Finally there is the idea of brotherhood (the *fraternité* of the French Revolution). The bulk of human history is the history of fratricide. In his *Philosophy of History* (and in this way I can break off the discussion at the point where I came in) Hegel defined history as an 'immense slaughterhouse'.[29] Can we disagree? In no country in the world can the democratic method last without becoming a habit. But can it become a habit without recognition of the bonds of kinship which unite all human beings in a common destiny? This recognition is all the more necessary now that every day we are made more aware of this common destiny. We ought, by the dim light of reason which still lights our path, to act accordingly.

# 2

# Representative and Direct Democracy

My starting point is an observation on which we can all agree: now that democracy has been extended to more areas of society than ever before, the call most frequently heard is for representative democracy to be complemented or actually replaced by direct democracy. This call is not new: it is implicit in the famous assertion of the father of modern democracy, Jean-Jacques Rousseau, that 'sovereignty cannot be represented' and that 'the English people think that they are free, but in this belief they are profoundly wrong. They are free only when electing members of Parliament. Once the election has been completed, they revert to a condition of slavery: they are nothing.'[1]

However Rousseau was also convinced that 'no true democracy has ever existed nor ever will', because it presupposes a number of conditions which are unlikely to prevail simultaneously. Firstly, it presupposes a state sufficiently small 'to make it possible to call the whole people together without difficulty and each citizen must be in a position to know all of his neighbours'. Secondly 'manners must be so simple that business will be kept to a minimum and thorny questions avoided.' Furthermore, it requires 'a considerable equality in fortune and in rank'. And finally there must be 'little or no luxury' (from which it might be inferred that it was Rousseau, not Marx, who inspired the politics of 'austerity'). Remember his conclusion: 'Were there such a thing as a nation of Gods, it would be a democracy. So perfect a form of government is not suited to mere men.'[2]

Even though two centuries have passed (and what centuries, for these centuries have actually seen liberal revolutions and socialist ones, and gave entire peoples for the first time the illusion of being destined for 'magnificent and progressive futures'), we have not become gods, but remained human beings. States have grown increasingly large and densely populated places, where no citizen is in a position to know all the others. Social customs have not become more simple, and as a result discussions get more thorny every day. Far from diminishing, the inequalities in wealth in the states that claim to be democratic (even if not in the Rousseauistic sense of the term) have steadily increased, and continue to be an outrage. Meanwhile luxury, which according to Rousseau 'corrupts both the rich and the poor, the rich through their possessions, the poor through their lust to possess',[3] has not disappeared (so much so that the intentionally provocative, but understandable, demands of some Italian terrorist groups include the insistence on the right to luxury).

Is then the call for an extension of representative democracy and for the introduction of direct democracy absurd? I do not believe it is. But to answer this question it is necessary first to clarify the terms of the debate.

Obviously, if by direct democracy is meant the participation of all citizens in all the decisions which concern them, the proposal is absurd. For everyone to make decisions on everything in the increasingly complex societies which exist in modern industrial nations is physically impossible. And it is also undesirable in human terms, i.e. from the point of view of the ethical and intellectual development of humanity. In his early writings, Marx had held up the total human being as the ultimate goal of the social evolution of the species. But the Rousseauistic individual called upon to participate in the political process from morning to night in order to exercise his rights as citizen would not be the total human being but the total citizen (a term coined by Dahrendorf with obvious polemical intent).[4] And the total citizen is on closer inspection merely another aspect, and a no less menacing one, of the total state. It is no coincidence that Rousseauistic democracy has often been interpreted as totalitarian democracy, in basic conflict with liberal democracy.

The total citizen and the total state are two sides of the same coin, because they have in common, even if in the first case it is considered from the people's point of view and in the other from that of the ruler, the same principle: that everything is political, in other words the reduction of all human interests to the interests of the *polis*, the integral politicization of humanity, the total transformation of human beings into citizens, the complete transposition of the private sphere into the public sphere, and so on.

I do not believe that someone who calls for direct democracy has such things in mind. It would not appear that Marx had this type of direct democracy in mind when he saw in the exercise of the power by the *Communards* in Paris the seed of a state organization different from that of the representative state (and particularly different from the Bonapartist state), even if the highly atypical experience of the Paris Commune, limited as it was in space and duration, could give rise to the illusion that it was possible and desirable to maintain even in normal times the state of continuous and impassioned mobilization which is possible and actually necessary in a period of the revolutionary transformation of society. (Perhaps the only type of human being for whom the term total citizen is appropriate is the revolutionary; but revolutions are not made by applying the ground rules of democracy.) But if this is so, when people use the formula 'from representative to direct democracy', what are they really asking for? Political slogans have the task of indicating an overall direction in which to progress, and it matters little if they are expressed in ambiguous and vague terms which are more liable to arouse certain emotions than to make certain realities concrete.

It is the task of theoretical criticism to identify and denounce solutions which can only exist on paper, to translate impressive formulas into feasible proposals, to distinguish the solid content in emotive rhetoric. If it is not too presumptuous, this is the task I have set myself in the following pages.

I will start with representative democracy. The first ambiguity we must clear up is whether 'representative democracy' means the same thing as the 'parliamentary state'. I propose to address this question straight away because many think that in criticizing the parliamentary state they have criticized representative democracy. I became aware of this in the course of the debate prompted by my articles on democracy and socialism, and carried on in journals and in dozens of platform discussions.[5] I finally had to recognize that it was almost always taken for granted that if someone criticized the parliamentary state it was at the same time a criticism of representative democracy.

Generically the expression 'representative democracy' means that collective deliberations, i.e. deliberations which concern the whole community, are taken not directly by its members, but by people elected for this purpose. Full stop. The parliamentary state is a particular application, even if it is historically a particularly relevant one, of the principle of representation; it is the type of state in which the central representative body (or at least central in theory, if not always in practice) to which all petitions are addressed and from which all decisions emanate is parliament. But everyone knows that even a presidential republic, like the United States, is not a parliamentary state but it is still generically a representative state.

Besides, there is no representative state in the world today whose principle of representation operates exclusively in parliament: the states which nowadays we usually call representative are regarded as such because the principle of representation has spread to other contexts where collective decisions are taken, i.e. boroughs, counties and in Italy, regions as well. In other words, a representative state is a state where the main political decisions are taken by elected representatives, irrespective of whether the body they form is parliament, the presidency, parliament in conjunction with regional councils or whatever.

In the same way that not every representative state is a parliamentary state, a parliamentary state may very well not be a representative state. If by democracy we understand, as we are meant to, a regime in which all adult citizens have political rights, one in which there is, to put it simply, universal suffrage, we know that historically parliaments came on the scene before the suffrage was extended, and hence for a long time parliaments were representative without being democratic. I would like to point out that in the expression 'representative democracy' it is as important to emphasize the adjective as the noun. While it is true that not every form of democracy is representative (hence the insistence on direct democracy), it is also true that not every representative state is democratic just by virtue of being representative. This is why I underline the fact that criticizing the parliamentary state does not imply criticism of representative democracy, since, if it is true that every democracy is representative, it is equally true that not every representative state is by definition a democracy, or that historically it has been one.

This leads to my next point. I have just said that criticism of the parliamentary state does not imply criticism of representative democracy. I must now add that not every criticism of representative democracy leads automatically to the advocacy of direct democracy. At this point the discussion gets complicated and I am forced to simplify, even at the risk of trivializing it. The complication derives from the fact that when I say that a person has the role of representing another person or a group of persons this expression is open to highly contrasting interpretations. The juridical, sociological and political science literature devoted to the concept, or rather the term, 'representation' is so enormous that even to give an account of the subject in its broadest outlines I would have to write an entire book.[6] To give some faint notion of the conceptual labyrinth that awaits anyone who tries to get to the bottom of what is meant by saying A represents B and then communicate the insight to others, I will simply point out that to say that the Pope is the representative of God on earth is not the same as saying Reagan represents the people of the United States. Then again, saying that Mr Jones represents a drug company is not the same as saying that the Right Honourable Smith represents a party in parliament.

Fortunately the only usage that is germane to this discussion is the last one. But even this usage is full of pitfalls. Suffice it to say that the age-old debate on political representation is dominated by at least two issues over which minds are deeply divided and which lead to diametrically opposed political positions. The first issue concerns the powers of the representative, the second what representation involves. For the sake of convenience it is customary to state that, once it is established that A is to represent B, the problem of representation has different solutions according to the different answers which are given to the questions '*How* does A represent B?' and '*What* is A representing?' The most common answers to these two questions are well known. To the first: A can represent B either in the role of 'delegate' or in the role of 'fiduciary', analagous to a trustee. If it is as a delegate, A is purely and simply a spokesman, an ambassador, an emissary, a messenger of those he represents, and thus the scope of the mandate is extremely restricted and revocable *ad nutum*. If, on the other hand, A is in the position of a fiduciary, this confers the power to act with a certain independence in the name of and on behalf of those represented. In as far as the judiciary enjoys their trust, A can use personal discretion in interpreting their interests. In this second case, A is said to represent B without a binding mandate, or, expressed in the terminology of constitutional theory, the relationship between A and B is not one of mandation. Even the second question (about 'what') admits two answers: A can represent B in respect of his general interests as a citizen, or alternatively in respect of particular interests as a worker, business executive, professional etc. Moreover it is important to note that the difference about 'what' is represented also has implications for 'who' is the representative.

If the representative is called upon to represent the general interests of the person represented it is not essential that he or she should be a member of the same professional category, in fact quite the reverse: an established feature common to most representative systems has been the formation of a specific category of professional representatives, i.e. professional politicians. On the other hand, when the representative is called upon to represent the specific interests of a social group, he or she normally belongs to the same professional group as those represented on the principle that workers can be effectively represented only by a worker, doctors by a doctor, teachers by a teacher, students by a student etc.

I do not think the reader will have missed the link between the representation of particular interests and the role of the delegate on the one hand, and the representation of general interests and the role of the fiduciary on the other. Usually the two things do indeed go hand in hand in this way. I will take an example familiar to Italians: student protest. It was the student power movements which first threw out their representative bodies on the grounds that the representatives were fiduciaries and not delegates and proceeded to impose via their assemblies the principle of the binding mandate. At the same time, it was clear that this was a case of organic representation, that is of particular interests in which the representative and those represented belong to the same social group.

The opposite occurs, however, in the political representation operating in most states based on a representative system. In most representative democracies the answer to 'who' the representative is, is that he is a fiduciary and not a delegate, and 'what' he represents are general rather than particular interests. (Moreover it is precisely because general and not particular interests are represented that there is a principle in force in democracies forbidding the use of binding mandates).

Having established this conceptual framework, I believe I am now in a position to specify what the term 'representation' connotes when we say that a system is representative and when people ordinarily talk about representative democracy. In such circumstances a representative means a person with two very specific attributes: someone who (a) enjoys the trust of the electorate by virtue of election, and so is responsible to them and therefore cannot be dismissed; and (b) who is not directly answerable to the electorate precisely because he is called upon to safeguard the general interests of civil society and not the particular interests of any one group.

In political elections where the representative system operates, a Communist worker does not vote for a non-Communist worker, but for a Communist even if he is not a worker. This means that the solidarity of the Party, and thus the vision of the general interests of the electorate, carries more weight than the solidarity of any one interest group and hence has priority over the consideration of particular interests. As I have already said, one result of this system is that representatives, in so far as they do not represent a specific interest group but are, in a manner of speaking, representatives of general interests, have come to form an interest group in themselves comprised of professional politicians (i.e. those who, to invoke the extremely apposite definition of Max Weber, do not only live *for* politics but live *by* politics).

I have emphasized these two basic features of representation because, in general, critiques of representative democracy focus precisely on these two aspects in the hope of achieving a more extensive, more complete, in a word, more democratic type of democracy. Two major strands can be clearly distinguished in these polemics. First there is the criticism of the prohibition against binding mandates – and hence of representation conceived as a fiduciary relationship – in the name of a more immediate link between representative and represented, along the lines of that which binds mandator to the mandatary in private law. Then there is the criticism of the representation of general interests by those who uphold the necessity for the sectional representation of the parti-cular interests of this or that social group.

Whoever is familiar with the history of this centuries-old dispute over the pros and cons of a representative system of politics knows well enough that these are the two central issues. Both form part of the tradition of socialist thought, or more precisely of the conception of democracy which emerged as socialist thinkers refined their critique of representative democracy, which they held to be the ideology peculiar to the most progressive wing of the bourgeoisie, as the 'bourgeois' ideology of democracy. Of the two issues, the first, i.e the call for the mandate from the electorate to be revoked on the grounds that the prohibition of the binding mandate is indefensible, stems directly from Marxist political thought. As is well known, it was Marx who went out of his way to highlight the fact that the Paris Commune 'filled all posts – administrative, judicial, and educational – by election on the basis of universal suffrage, subject to the right of recall at any time by the same electors'.[7]

The principle was taken up and repeatedly stressed by Lenin, starting with *State and Revolution*,[8] and became a guiding principle of various Soviet constitutions. Article 105 of the present Consti-tution reads: 'The deputy is obliged to consult electors about his activity and the activity of the Soviet. The deputy who has not shown himself to be worthy of the trust of the electors can immediately be deprived of his mandate at any moment by a majority decision of the electors made in accordance with the procedures laid down by the law.' This principle has been passed on to most constitutions of people's democracies (which is the opposite of what has happened in most constitutions in Western democracies, such as the Italian one, where Article 67 reads 'Every member of Parliament represents the

Nation and exercises his function without the restrictions of a mandate.')

In contrast, the second issue, concerning the representation of sectional interests, or organic representation, is a feature of late nineteenth-century English socialist thought and in particular of that current of thought which stemmed from the guild socialism of Hobson and Cole. The fundamental institutional reform they proposed consisted in breaking the state down into corporations, leaving only its territorial integrity, and the establishment of functional representation (i.e. of formally constituted and recognized particular interests) alongside the territorial representation which was the responsibility of the classic parliamentary state, a form of government which had after all originated in England.

I must stress that neither of these proposals to renew the political system has the effect of transforming representative into direct democracy. Certainly, the second we have mentioned does not, for it confines itself to substituting one form of representation for another. It is also debatable whether the functional representation of interests, even if it has been proposed by political movements on the Left, is more democratic than territorial representation as carried out by those bodies for the aggregation of general interests which are the parties of today.

In Italy we cannot forget that the only attempt made so far to substitute functional representation, for representation through political parties was carried out, no matter how ineffectually, by the Fascists with the *camera dei fasci* and the *camera delle corporazioni*.[9] For my part, I remember how in the years immediately after the First World War proposals for constitutional reform were aired not only by some socialist groups but also by the Catholic Party, which moved towards basing representation on interests. The dangers for the subsequent development of democracy and for civil liberties were spotted by two liberal writers, namely Einaudi and Ruffini. (Einaudi wrote: 'It is necessary to state that we, who are opposed to these self-styled modern legislative principles, have the duty to put on record that all these representations of particular interests, all these joint assemblies constitute a staggering regression back to medieval forms of political representation, back to those forms which modern parliamentary systems discarded as part of their progressive improvement'. He added: 'To confer on bodies representing the professions a decision-making function is to replace general interests by vested interests, and moreover sanctions egoism and the abuse of power)'.[10]

This is not meant to imply that I accept that our parliaments are devoted exclusively to the general interest. I would never dream of saying such a thing. One of the plagues of our parliamentary system, which seems to thrive on condemnation, is the proliferation of what are called in Italian *leggine*, or 'little laws', which are passed precisely to benefit a small minority as a result of successful lobbying by pressure groups which have, in the worst sense of the word, corporate interests. But the point is that this is indeed a plague and not something positive; it is one of the degenerative aspects of parliaments which ought to be put right and not made worse.

The problem of organic representation was taken up again in the course of the deliberations of the Constituent Assembly, after the Second World War. It was resolved with the creation of a kind of constitutional limbo in the form of the National Council for Economy and Work, which was given a merely consultative function that in fact it has never performed either after it was constituted, or since its recent resuscitation.

Let us be clear on this: there is nothing inherently wrong with organic or sectional representation. There are situations where it is not only desirable but inevitable. It is obvious that a university faculty committee should be composed of faculty lecturers rather than of the representatives of political parties. However what is less obvious is that student representatives or members of the administration do not take part in such meetings with the same rights, and that when they do any shortcomings in the functioning of democracy are not due to the representation being sectional, but to its not being sectional enough. But a faculty committee, like a factory committee, performs its proper function and makes its own decisions within a clearly circumscribed and technical sphere, i.e. in a sphere which has nothing to do with the general and non-technical sphere that representative political bodies have to deal with. What is open to criticism is not sectional representation as such, but sectional representation which has been extended outside its proper sphere.

Thus there can be no objection to students being represented by students in schools, or workers by workers in factories. But once the context changes to where what is at stake are the interests of the citizen and not those of this or that interest group, citizens should be represented by citizens who are distinguished from each other on the grounds, not of the interest groups they represent, but of the different general visions they have developed which inform the way they conceive the problems. (These are general visions which each possesses by virtue of membership, not of this or that interest group, but of this or that political movement).

Certainly the arrangement whereby the representative is revocable comes much closer to direct democracy than the one where the representative is independent of any binding mandate. In fact the umbilical cord which keeps the delegate tied to the electing body is never cut at all. But even in this case it is impossible to talk about direct democracy in the true sense of the term. For there to be direct democracy in the true sense of the term, that is in the sense in which direct means that individuals participate personally in the deliberations which concern them, there should be no intermediary at all between those who make the decisions and those affected by them. Even the revocable delegate is an intermediary, not least because no matter how bound he or she is by the instructions received from those represented, in practice there is some room for manoeuvre. If there were no leeway for any of the delegates who have to reach a collective decision, then collective decision-making would be impossible. Moreover a delegate cannot be recalled at a moment's notice and replaced by another without the risk of paralysing the negotiations.

The person who does act on the basis of strict instructions is the spokesman, the messenger, or in international diplomacy, the ambassador. But such inflexibility of instructions is not at all typical of the way collective bodies work. If anything, it is typical of bodies regulated on a hierarchical basis: namely, structures in which power moves from the top downwards and not from the bottom up, and which are thus much better adapted to autocratic systems than to democratic ones. This is true if for no other reason than that someone holding superior rank in a hierarchy can give strict instructions to a subordinate in the hierarchy much more easily than an assembly. The latter may succeed, even if only at the cost of enormous effort, in formulating policy decisions, but is hardly ever able to translate these into orders (and where there are not orders but policies a mandate can only be binding on paper).

In any case, if representation by mandate is not really direct democracy, it is a half-way house between representative democracy and direct democracy. This prompts me to reiterate the point I made earlier: between pure representative and pure direct democracy there is not the qualitative leap which the advocates of direct democracy believe, as if a watershed separated the two and once you had passed over it the landscape changed completely. No: the historical forms of representative and direct democracy are so many and varied that one cannot pose the issue in terms of either/or, as if there was only one possible version of each. The problem of the transition from one to the other can only be posed in terms of a continuum, where it is difficult to say at which point one finishes and the other begins.

A democratic system involving revocable representatives is a form of representative democracy in that it allows for representatives, but approximates to direct democracy in that they are revocable. It is an amphibious species, and history, which tends to proceed by circuitous routes (in contrast to nature which it used to be said follows the shortest route), offers us innumerable examples of its kind. Precisely because there is a sliding scale of intermediary forms connecting the extreme version of representative democracy to the extreme version of direct democracy, any fully fledged system of democracy can usually accommodate all of them, each permutation adapted to different situations and different needs, because they are, being appropriate to different situations and different needs, perfectly compatible with each other. This implies that in reality representative and direct democracy are not two alternative systems, in the sense that where there is one there cannot be the other, but are two systems that can mutually complement each other. One could sum up the situation by saying that in a mature system of democracy both forms of democracy are necessary but they are not, taken on their own, self-sufficient.

The inadequacies of direct democracy become obvious when one considers that the mechanisms available to direct democracy in the true sense of the word are twofold: the citizens' assembly deliberating without intermediaries, and the referendum. No complex system like a modern state can function with either of these alone, or even with both in conjunction.

The citizens' assembly, the form of democracy which Rousseau had in mind, is an institution which, as Rousseau knew full well himself, can exist only in a small community. This was the case of the classical model *par excellence*, Athens in the fifth and sixth centuries BC, when there were only a few thousand citizens and their assembly, allowing for those who were absent of their own free will or otherwise, could all stand together in the agreed venue. (Indeed Glotz claims it was rare to see more than two or three thousand citizens, even if, on the hillside where the normal assemblies were usually held, there was room for, again according to Glotz, twenty-five thousand people standing and for eighteen thousand people sitting on benches).[11]

Nowadays there are no longer city-states, except for a handful of cases which are so exceptional that they can in this context be safely ignored. What's more, the cities within states have become somewhat bigger than the Athens of Pericles or the Geneva of Rousseau.

We have, it is true, divided them up into voting wards, or we are in the process of doing so. It may be true that in the initial stages of mobilizing political involvement in a district or ward, when local committees spring up more or less spontaneously, it is appropriate to talk of direct democracy (direct, yes, but very limited in quantitative terms). Nevertheless it is just as true – due to the natural tendency inherent in the transition from a movement at its inception, or *statu nascenti* as Alberoni puts it, to its institutionalization, from its spontaneous phase to the inevitable phase of organization – that immediately provisions have been made covering the legitimation and regulation of the grass-roots participation, the participation has by definition taken the form of representative democracy. Even voting wards are governed not by an assembly of citizens, but by their representatives.

As for the referendum, which is the only mechanism of direct democracy which can be applied concretely and effectively in most advanced democracies, this is an extraordinary expedient suited only for extraordinary circumstances. No one can imagine a state that can be governed via continuous appeals to the people: taking into account the approximate number of laws which are drafted in Italy every year, we would have to call a referendum on average once a day. That is unless we take seriously the science-fiction scenario whereby citizens could transmit their vote to an electronic brain just by pressing a button in the comfort of their own homes.[12]

Yet there is no doubt that we are witnessing the extension of the process of democratization. If it was necessary to identify the most obvious and interesting symptoms of a society in a state of political expansion, like Italy, one of the first things to point out would be the success achieved by the calls for participation in ever new areas of decision-making. I apologize for being a little simplistic, but power can only flow in two directions: either it is descending, moving from top to bottom, or ascending, from bottom to top. In modern states a typical example of the former is bureaucratic power, and of the latter political power, where by political power is meant power exercised at all levels, local, regional, state, in the name of and on behalf of the citizen, or rather of the individual as citizen.

Right now the process of democratization, i.e. the expansion of ascending power, is spreading from the sphere of political relations, i.e. dealings in which individuals are considered in their role as citizen, to the sphere of social relations, where individuals are considered in terms of the various functions they may have and the roles they may play in specific situations. These can include those of parent, child, spouse, impresario, worker, teacher, student, of doctor and patient, officer and private, civil servant and supplicant, producer and consumer, director of a public utility and customer and so on.

I would characterize the situation as follows: if one can talk nowadays of a process of democratization, it does not consist, as many people often erroneously make out, in the transition from representative democracy to direct democracy, but from what is strictly speaking political democracy to social democracy. In other words ascending power, which hitherto was almost entirely confined to the macrocosm of politics at a national level (and to some small, minute, politically irrelevant voluntary associations) is spreading to various spheres of civil society, ranging from the school to the factory. I speak of the school and the factory because they epitomize places where most members of modern society spend the majority of their lives. I intentionally leave out of account the Church or the Churches, because religious society is neither political nor civil, though even religious society is being thrown into turmoil by the same pressing issue of democratization.

In short, we can say that the way modern society is developing is not to be understood as the emergence of a new type of democracy but rather as a process in which quite traditional forms of democracy, such as representative democracy, are infiltrating new spaces, spaces occupied until now by hierarchic or bureaucratic organizations.

Seen from this angle I believe that it is justified to talk of a genuine turning-point in the evolution of democratic institutions which can be summed up in a simple formula: from the democratization of the state to the democratization of society.

It is easy enough to understand that, historically, the advent of political democracy preceded the advent of social democracy, if we see politics as the sphere in which the decisions are taken that most affect the community as a whole.

Once political democracy had been achieved it was realized that the political sphere is itself part of the much wider sphere formed by society as a whole, and that there is no political decision which is not conditioned or actually determined by what happens in civil society. Furthermore, people appreciated that it is one thing to democratize the state, which can be achieved largely through the establishment of a parliamentary system, and quite another to democratize society, with the result that a democratic state may well exist in a society where most institutions, from family to school, from business to the management of social services, are not run democratically. This gives rise to the question which typifies better than any other the current phase of democratic evolution in countries which are politically speaking already democratic: is it possible for a democratic state to survive in a non-democratic society? This can also be formulated in another way: political democracy has been and continues to be necessary to prevent a nation falling prey to a despotic regime. But is it enough?

I have already mentioned as an indication of this radical change the fact that until very recently whenever people wanted to test the advance made by democracy in a particular country they took as an index of progress the extension of political rights from restricted suffrage to universal suffrage, thus taking as the main barometer of democracy the spread of the right to participate, even if only indirectly, in forming the bodies responsible for political decisions. There is no more progress possible in this direction now that suffrage has been enlarged to include women and the age limit has been lowered to eighteen.

Nowadays, if an indicator of democratic progress is needed it cannot be provided by the number of people who have the right to vote, but the number of contexts outside politics where the right to vote is exercised. A laconic but effective way of putting it is to say that the criterion for judging the state of democratization achieved in a given country should no longer be to establish 'who' votes, but 'where' they can vote (and it should be pointed out that I mean here by 'voting' the most typical and common way of participating, but do not intend to limit participation to casting a vote).

From now on when we pose the question whether democracy has made any progress over the last few years in Italy, we must inquire, not how many more electors there are, but how many more spaces there are where the citizen can exercise the right to vote. An example of such a democratic reform is the setting up of schools' councils which involve the participation of parents. (In contrast the similar provision for the election of student representatives to university committees is to be considered an inadequate and abortive move, abortive because it is inadequate.)

We must face up to the fact that this is a process which has only just started and we have no idea how it will develop and how far it will go. We do not know if it is destined to continue or to come to a halt, to progress slowly or in bursts. There are some encouraging signs and others less so. Parallel to the need for self-rule there is the desire not to be ruled at all and to be left in peace. The effects of an excess of politicization can be that the private sphere reasserts itself. The other side of the coin to extending politicization into many areas of decision-making is political apathy. The price exacted by the *engagement* of the few is often the indifference of the many. A corollary of the political activism of the famous and not so famous leaders in history is the conformism of the masses.

Nothing corrodes the spirit of the politically active citizen more than *qualunquismo*, the political indifference of those who only seek to cultivate their gardens. This is a notion that had already been expressed very clearly by classical writers. As Pericles put it in a famous sentence passed down to us by Thucydides, 'We do not say that a man who takes no interest in politics is a man who minds his own business, we say that he has no business here at all.'[13] Rousseau was equally convinced of this and stated that,'As soon as the public service of the State ceases to be the main concern of the citizens, and they find it easier to serve the State with their purses than with their persons, ruin draws near.' Or as he put it in one of those pithy phrases so characteristic of him, 'As soon as a man, thinking of the affairs of the State, says: "They don't concern me", it is time to conclude that the State is lost.'[14]

In any event one thing is certain: the process of democratization has not even begun to scratch the surface of the two great blocks of descending and hierarchical power in every complex society, big business and public administration. And as long as these two blocks hold out against the pressures exerted from below, the democratic transformation of society cannot be said to be complete. We cannot even say whether this transformation is even possible. We can only say that if the advance of democracy will in future be measured in terms of the infiltration of spaces still occupied by non-democratic centres of power, these spaces are so numerous and so large, and their importance so great, that a fully realized democracy, assuming such a goal to be not only desirable but possible, is still a long way off.

But at the same time, changing the depth of focus from the state to civil society forces us to take note of the fact that there are other centres of power besides the state. Modern societies are not monocratic but polycratic, something that can easily strand the unsuspecting on the quick sands of pluralism. One thing is sure: from the moment we abandon the limited perspective of the political system and extend our field of vision to include the society which underlies it, we come up against centres of power which exist within the state but are not directly identified with the state. Inevitably it is at this point that the problem of democracy encounters the problem of pluralism, and subsumes it, so to speak.[15]

But before considering this aspect, a preliminary warning is called for. Often in the course of the recent discussion of pluralism the opinion has been expressed that a pluralistic society and a democratic society are one and the same thing. It is claimed that since entities should not be multiplied unnecessarily, a maxim which applies not just to well-governed states (as is the case of Italy which is notorious not only for turning the provisional into the only element of continuity, but considering indispensible only what is super-fluous!), but to philosophy as well, the concept of pluralism serves merely to foment the passion of intellectuals for scholastic disputes. This is not true: the concept of democracy and the concept of plural-ism are, as a logician would say, not coterminous. There is no reason why there should not exist a non-democratic pluralist society and a non-pluralist democracy.

As a paradigm of the former the mind immediately turns to feudal Europe, which is the historically most striking example of a society made up of several power centres, often in competition with each other, and a very weak central authority. We would hesitate to call it a 'state' in the modern sense of the word, since we apply this term to territorial entities which came about precisely as a result of the dissolution of medieval society. Feudal society is a pluralistic society but is not a democratic society: it is a network of oligarchies.

To exemplify the second, the democracy of classical times again comes to the rescue, in which all public activity took place in the *polis* and democracy, being, as stated already, direct, there was no intermediary body between the individual and the city. Rousseau surely had classical democracy and direct democracy in mind when he condemned 'partial societies' as injurious to the formation of the general will because – as he saw it – the opinion which would eventually prevail would be a particular opinion. So he proceeded to set out the conditions of a non-pluralistic democracy and went as far as declaring that pluralism would be the ruin of democracy.

If the two concepts of democracy and of pluralism do not coincide, then to clarify the relationship between them, far from being futile, plays a vital role in any attempt to take stock of precisely how democratization is or is not developing. That our societies, in contrast to the classical *polis*, have several centres of power is an undeniable fact. What follows from this fact is simply that, unlike what happened in democracies in the ancient world, democracies in the modern world have to come to terms with pluralism. Pluralism is not primarily a theory but first and foremost an objective situation which is part and parcel of our lives. It is no invention of Catholics or communists if present-day Italian society is pluralistic, but a reality which Catholics and communists, and even those who are neither, are seeking to interpret, admittedly in their own particular way, all trying to predict the pattern of its progression (so as not to be left behind or to do something to counteract it). For the sake of convenience the effects of pluralism on Italian society can be said to operate on three levels: economic, political and ideological.

There is no doubt that on each of these three levels Italian society breaks down into a cluster of opposing groups, which serve as a focal point for tensions, often profound in nature, so that they are continually being rent by explosive conflicts in a permanent process of disintegration and recomposition. There is pluralism at an economic level, where we have a market economy still partially intact and big businesses are still in competition with each other, while at the same time there is a public sector distinct from the private sector, with everything that implies. There is political pluralism, the effect of several parties or political movements vying with each other to gain power over the state or society, either through winning votes or by other means. Ideological pluralism obtains from the moment there is not just one doctrine of the state but various currents of thought, various visions of the world, various political programmes which have free reign and are reflected in a public opinion which is far from homogenous or uniform. It is a fact of everyday experience that on all these three levels of Italian society discord prevails, and to a degree which to outside observers must at times seem quite excessive.

So what does it mean to say that democracy must come to terms with pluralism? It means that the democracy of a modern state has no alternative but to be a pluralistic democracy. Let us examine the reasons. What democratic and pluralist theory have in common is that they are two different critiques of the abuse of power, not incompatible but in fact complementary and convergent. They represent two different, but not necessarily alternative, remedies against the excessive concentration of power. Democratic theory is directed against autocratic power, i.e. power from above, and maintains that the remedy to this type of power can only be power from below. Pluralist theory is directed against monocratic power, i.e. power concentrated in the hands of one person, and maintains that the remedy for this type of power lies in its proper distribution.

The disparity between these two remedies stems from the fact that autocratic and monocratic power are not the same thing. To use our previous examples, Rousseau's republic is both democratic and autocratic, while feudal society is both autocratic and polycratic. But if autocratic and monocratic power are not identical, two other ideal-types of state become possible: the state which is both monocratic and autocratic, the most well-known historical example being absolute monarchy, and the state which is both democratic and polycratic, which I see to be the essential characteristic of modern democracy.

In other words, democracy in modern states is characterized by the struggle against the abuse of power on two parallel fronts: against power from above in the name of power from below, and against the concentration of power in the name of the distribution of power. Moreover it is not difficult to explain which objective reasons make this two-pronged counter-attack necessary. Where direct democracy is possible the state can very well be ruled by a sole centre of power, such as the citizens' assembly. Where direct democracy, because of the vastness of the territory to be governed, the number of inhabitants, and the host of problems demanding solutions, is impossible and it becomes necessary to resort to representative democracy, the guarantee against the abuse of power cannot derive solely from control from below, which is indirect, but must also rely on reciprocal arrangements between groups which represent various interests and are expressed in various political movements which contend with each other for the temporary and peaceful exercise of power.

As has been said on many occasions, the defect of representative democracy compared with direct democracy, namely that it tends to produce small oligarchies in the form of party committees, can only be corrected by the existence of a whole range of oligarchies in open competition with each other. It is all the better if these small oligarchies become steadily less oligarchic with the progressive democratization of civil society due to greater levels of participation, and the conquest of the various centres of power in civil society, thereby ensuring that power is not only distributed but also controlled.

Finally pluralism has the advantage of making us aware of a basic trait of modern democracy when compared to the democracy of classical times: the freedom, even the licence, we enjoy to express dissent. This fundamental feature of modern democracy is based on the principle that dissent, as long as it is kept within certain limits which are established by the so-called rules of the game, does not undermine a society but underpins it, and that a society in which dissent is not allowed is either doomed or already dead. Among the thousands of items which can be read on these issues, I have come across nothing more convincing to my mind than an article by Franco Alberoni, published in *Corriere della Sera* on 9 January 1977, called 'Democracy Means Dissent'. Alberoni's piece was prompted by a televized round-table discussion in which some well-known personalities argued that a democratic society comes about when it can rely on the consensus of all its members. His reaction was

'Far from it'. He went on to say, 'Democracy is a political system which presupposes dissent. It demands consent on one point only: on the rules of competition.' This is so because in the West democracy 'means a political system in which there is not consent but dissent, competition, contest'.

As often happens when someone reacts to a mistaken argument, Alberoni errs by going to the other extreme. It is obvious that democracy is not only characterized by dissent but also by consent (and not just on the rules of the game). He meant that a democratic system does not require the unanimous consent which totalitarian democracies claim exists, willingly or unwillingly (but can a consent achieved through force still be called consent?). Such regimes, as Alberoni quite rightly says, instead of allowing those who think differently the right of opposition, want to reduce them to the role of faithful subjects. But precisely what is implied by majority consent is a minority of dissenters.

What do we do with these dissenters, once we accept that unanimous consent is impossible and that where it is claimed to exist it must have been been organized, manipulated, manoeuvred and is thus fictitious, that it is the consent of those, in Rousseau's famous phrase, who are obliged to be free? Besides, what value has consensus in a situation where dissent is forbidden, where there is no choice between agreeing and disagreeing, where agreement is obligatory and even rewarded, and disagreement is not only forbidden but actually punished? Is this still consent or merely passive acceptance of the rule of the strongest? If consent is not freely given what difference is there between agreement and the obedience owed to a superior demanded by a hierarchic system? But then, if we cannot accept unanimous consent as a more perfect form of consent, and hence recognize that a system founded on consent inevitably contains dissent, what is to be done, I pose the question once more, with the dissenters? Do we suppress them or let them live? If we let them live, do we lock them away or let them move around freely, do we gag them or keep them among us as free citizens?

It is useless deluding ourselves: the acid test of a democratic system is the type of answer we give to these questions. I do not mean by this that democracy is a system not founded on consent but dissent. I mean that in a political system founded on a consensus which is not imposed from above, some form of dissent is inevitable and that only where dissent is free to express itself is consensus real, and furthermore that only where consensus is real can a system justly claim to be democratic. For this reason I maintain that a necessary relationship exists between democracy and dissent, because, and I repeat, once it is accepted that democracy signifies a real consensus and not a fictitious one, the only possiblity open to us of assessing the reality of the consensus is to assess the degree of its opposite. But how can we assess it if we prevent it?

I have no intention of broaching here the problem of the dialectical relationship between consent and dissent, let alone the question of the limits of dissent that must necessarily exist in all political systems. While there is no system in which dissent does not show through despite all the limitations imposed by the authorities to conceal it, equally there can be no system without limits to dissent despite the proclamations of freedom of opinion, of the press, etc. Reality does not know ideal-types but only various approximations to one or other ideal-type.

But there is surely a difference between allowing all forms of political organization except ones which are considered subversive (and which are those which do not respect the rules of the game), and banning all forms of political organization except the official one (which not only imposes the rules of the game, but also the only way the game is to be played). Between the two extremes there are scores of intermediary forms. Between pure despotism at one extreme and pure democracy at the other there are scores of political systems which are more or less despotic and more or less democratic. And it may be that a democracy with some degree of social control could turn into a despotism, just as a despotism which relaxes its grip might evolve into a democracy. But a discriminating criterion exists, namely the amount of space reserved for dissent.

It should now be clear why I connected the problem of pluralism with the problem of dissent. On close inspection it turns out that only in a pluralist society is dissent possible: not just possible but vital.

It all fits together: if we follow the causal chain through starting at the other end, freedom of dissent presupposes a pluralistic society, a pluralistic society allows a greater distribution of power, a greater distribution of power opens the door to the democratization of civil society, and eventually democratization of civil society extends and integrates political democracy.

Thus I feel I have pointed out, with a number of imprecisions and shortcomings of which I am only too aware, the path which could lead to the extension of democracy without necessarily ending up in direct democracy. Personally I am convinced that this is the right path, even if it is fraught with danger. Yet I am also convinced that a good democrat should neither have delusions about achieving the best, nor be resigned to accepting the worst.

# 3

# The Constraints of Democracy

To embark on a discussion of '*alternative* politics' we must realize we are dealing with a phrase eroded by years of use and abuse, and, like all political slogans, more pregnant with evocative power than with precise meaning. Thus it is essential to consider not just possible *new* themes and *new* stategies, but first and foremost the rules of the game in which the political contest unfolds in a given historical situation.

The issue of the rules of the game is extremely important, and we can only leave it out of account at the risk of being faced by a question which is badly formulated and hence unresolvable, for at least two reasons. Above all, because what distinguishes a democratic system from any other is not merely the fact that it has particular rules of the game (every system has them in varying degrees of clarity and complexity), but that centuries of being asserted and challenged have made them more elaborate than the rules of other systems and that they are by now almost universally set forth in constitutions, as in Italy. I have stated on other occasions, and I will never tire of repeating it, that it is impossible to ever understand anything about democracy until it is realized that a democratic system nowadays signifies first and foremost a set of procedural rules, among which majority rule is the main, but not the only one.[1] By this I do not mean that for a government to be good it is enough for it to respect the rules of the democratic game. I merely mean that in our particular historical situation political contest is fought out according to certain rules and that respect for these rules forms, apart from anything else, the basis of the legitimacy of the whole system, a basis that so far, despite everything, is still inviolate. Thus those who raise the possibility of an alternative politics cannot avoid expressing their verdict on these rules, or stating whether they accept them or not, what they intend to replace them with if they do not accept them, and so forth.

I have the impression that in general the Left does not have clear ideas about the importance and nature of the 'rules of democracy' and whether to reform or replace them (with the exception of those who reject a regulated contest for a form of struggle that does not preclude terrorist acts and naked violence). I will give two examples. In a famous article (famous because it gave rise to a debate which went on for months and resulted in a book),[2] Althusser wrote that the party 'will respect the rules of the game in as far as they concern what its protagonists consider, according to classical legal principles, the sphere of politics'. But he adds immediately afterwards that 'the destruction of the bourgeois state does not mean the suppression of all its ground-rules, but a profound transformation of its apparatus.'[3] This is surely a rather vague statement. There is no question, according to Althusser, of suppressing all the rules of the game. Fine: but would he be so kind as to tell us which will be suppressed and which will not? Elsewhere I have expressed my relief that not all the democratic ground-rules will be abolished, but also my apprehension about not being told in advance which are the good ones to be retained and which bad ones will be done away with.[4] However, in as compact and coherent a system as democracy, where the procedures which have brought it into being have stood the test of centuries and created a tightly knit mesh of institutions, can one distinguish with such certainty between the rules worth maintaining and those we ought to discard? Shall we keep universal suffrage but not freedom of opinion? Freedom of opinion but not a multi-party system? A multi-party system but not the legal protection of civil rights? When it comes down to it, asserting that not all the rules of the game will be suppressed is a way of avoiding the need to state unambiguously a point of view on the crucial question posed by the rules of the game themselves, and more than anything else betrays the absolute lack of any ideas as to its possible solution.

A second example of the Left's vagueness on this issue is provided by a recent article by A. Rosa, which raises several interesting points and which I hope perhaps to discuss more fully on another occasion. In it he writes that the democratic system has rules which are 'in practice incontrovertible', but he condemns the fact that they have been turned into absolutes, considering this 'unwarranted'. He goes on to argue that 'democracy, precisely because it is a *system of mediocrities*, cannot make itself out to be an absolute or an end in itself . . ., it is a *game* whose defining feature is that it allows its own rules to be called into question. *If it does not it is already something else.*'[5] That even the rules of the game can be modified is indisputable and any good democrat could not help but agree. The proof of this is that all democratic institutions have procedures for the revision of their own constitutional norms and that historically such modifications have occurred. As a result, not all democratic constitutions have the same rules (think, for example, of the difference between a presidential and parliamentary form of government). In fact some rules have been added only in a second or third stage of the evolution of such constitutions, such as those which regulate the constitutionality of legislation, rules which in fact have not been universally adopted. But to agree with the thesis that even the rules of the game can be changed does not bring us a fraction closer to solving the most difficult problem of all: if all rules can be changed, since not all of them *can* be changed in practice, which can be changed and which cannot? To quote the usual example (usual, but in this case anything but trite): can a majority decision alter the rule of majority decisions? In simple terms: if a parliamentary majority decides, as has already happened in history, to abolish the parliamentary system and confer the power to make decisions binding on the whole community to a leader or a small oligarchy, is the resulting system still a democracy just because it has been instituted democratically? Of course, if a democracy is not prepared to call into question its own ground-rules, 'it is already something else.' But does it not become even more manifestly 'something else' if certain rules, such as the rule of the majority, are called into question? And so is there not a problem even more basic than that of the important one concerning the degree to which a democratic system is self-correcting, namely whether there are limits beyond which the process of continuous revision cannot go; and if there are, and I have no doubt they exist, what are they?

The second reason why a discussion of the issues and strategies of an 'alternative politics' makes it necessary to raise the question of the rules of the game derives from the inextricable link that sooner or later must be acknowledged to exist between the accepted rules of the political game as they stand, on the one hand, and the subjects who are the protagonists of the game and the ploys available to them to win it, on the other. To stay within the metaphor, there is an inextricable link which connects the rules of the game to the players and their moves. More specifically, what a game actually consists of is a set of rules which establish who the players are and how they are to play, with the result that once a system of rules is formulated for the game this also lays down who can be the players and the moves they are allowed. It is open to anyone to prefer a game in which the two contenders do not only punch but also kick each other, as long as it is realized that what is being proposed is simply a different game, namely free-style wrestling instead of boxing. (Moreover it would be inconceivable for anyone – anyone, that is, who did not want to be considered mad – to invent and promote a game in which one of the competitors was only allowed to punch while the other could also kick: yet in political debate even this occurs.)

In the democratic political game – where a fully legal democratic system is taken to be a system whose legitimacy depends on public consent periodically confirmed by the exercise of universal suffrage in free elections – it is laid down who the main players are, namely the parties (in the Italian system even this is prescribed in the Constitution in Article 49); and the main form of participating in politics for the vast majority of those who make up the nation is also laid down, namely elections. It is a question of take it or leave it. There is a saying in Italian to the effect that you can either eat the food you've been offered or take a running jump.[6] You are perfectly entitled to refuse what is given as long as you know that it means jumping out of the window and that you might break your neck: it is not like walking calmly out of the door. In short, the rules of the game, the players and their moves form a whole which cannot be broken down into separate units. Game theory distinguishes constitutive rules from regulatory rules: whereas the latter confine themselves to the regulation of activities which human beings pursue independently of the existence of rules, such as feeding themselves, making love, or walking in the street, the latter actually give rise to the behaviour they cover. In general the rules of games are constitutive, since the obligation to move the knight in a particular way does not exist outside the rules of chess.[7] But many rules of the political game are equally constitutive: electoral behaviour does not exist outside the laws which institute and regulate elections. Human beings make love irrespective of the norms of civil law which regulate marriage, but they do not vote unless there is an electoral law. In this sense the rules of the game, the players and the moves are interdependent because they owe their very existence to the rules. It follows from this that it is impossible to accept the rules but reject the players and propose different moves. Or rather it is possible as long as it is realized that it means jumping out of the window and not leaving by the door. What is absurd, or to say the least futile, is to long for a form of politics with different players and moves without realizing that to achieve this means changing the rules which provided for and created those players and laid down their moves even down to the last details. Like it or not, this is the only realistic way of formulating the issue open to a 'New Left', if such a thing still exists.

These reflections on the close relationship between rules, players and behaviour enable us to understand why the *annus mirabilis* of student power, 1968 (since we are talking about the New Left we cannot avoid referring to 1968), marked such an important break with what had gone before. In fact not only did new players emerge (the groups, the factions, the student movement in general) instead of parties in the traditional sense of the term, not only did it invent a new type of politics for the new players to perform, using assemblies, demonstrations and street agitation, the occupation of public buildings, the disruption of classes and academic meetings, but it also repudiated some of the basic rules of a democratic system, starting with elections (with the abolition of representative bodies, which were disparagingly called 'mini-parliaments') and with representation without mandate, installing in their place the principles of direct democracy and the binding mandate. Why this radical break only produced a series of crises and no transformation of the Italian political scene (and probably made it worse) is not a problem that can be discussed here. One of the reasons is certainly the feebleness of the alternatives proposed to the existing rules of the game, or rather precisely the lack of any alternative other than that of reducing politics to a trial of strength on the premiss that the only alternative to regulated political contest is the victory of the strongest.

It is now an incontrovertible fact that no transformation was brought about in Italy, and that democracy, with all the problems which accompany a system in a process of slow deterioration, was able to hold its ground, despite the vast territory completely overrun by the enemy and his undeniable vitality. Its resistence was weak, and is growing steadily weaker, but it resisted nonetheless. When I say that it resisted despite its defects, I mean that its principal protagonists, the traditional parties, continued to survive and to win over the vast majority of public opinion, notwithstanding the curses, complaints and grumbles which could be heard. The electoral 'rites' continued to take place at regular intervals, indeed they multiplied as administrations changed with greater rapidity, and on top of that since 1974 there have also been referendums. Abstentionism has increased, but not alarmingly, and in any case political apathy is in no way a symptom of crisis in a democratic system, but usually a sign of good health – that is, if political apathy is interpreted not as the rejection of a system but as benevolent indifference. In any case the parties which thrive in a political system where there is regularly a high degree of abstention, as is the case of American parties, could not care less if people do not go to vote. Quite the reverse: the fewer people vote, the less pressure they are under. Even Italian parties are only pretending to be concerned by the growing rate of abstentions. Or at least they are not concerned at abstentionism in itself, which leaves them freer to pursue their daily manoeuvres, but at the fact that abstentions work to the advantage of the opposition, or in concrete terms that the voters of their party are more likely to abstain than those of other parties.

On the other hand, just think of the number of revolutionary groups that formed in those years (where 'revolutionary' is totally appropriate in the sense that they were challenging not only the traditional players and their style of play, but the rules of the game themselves). How many have survived being dissolved, reformed and dissolved again in an endless process of realignment? Those who, at a certain point, wanted to pursue political goals outside the party system, were forced to set up a new party, like the Radical Party,[8] which in spite of its novelty is a party like all the others. The same was done, albeit with less success, by some extra-parliamentary groups which resigned themselves, almost out of necessity, to forming ephemeral parties with a scant following, while some of their founders, politicians for reasons of passion and vocation, preferred to find a home in one or other of the established parties. It is only too natural that the mediocre electoral results of these new parties have fuelled the temptation or illusion of alternative politics, of finding new paths to the political forum. The fact that these paths have yet to get them very far highlights the close connection I have stressed in this chapter between these new strategies and the logic of a system which allows them very little leeway. The same argument holds for the trade unions, which also form part of a pre-established system corresponding to the confrontation politics of capitalism. It is a system with its own rules, such as the right to strike and collective bargaining, and which is difficult to bypass or replace without totally changing it. But here too, the New Left has failed to outline clearly an alternative system, invoking not so much new forms of association as the working class as a whole, and appealing less for new structures of organization than the disappearance of all organization, for so-called 'spontaneous action', one of the many myths of the working-class Left. In socialist systems the trade union loses its *raison d'être* because these societies are neither capitalist nor are they based on conflict. Poland is a case apart, and it is difficult to predict how things will turn out.

The reference to trade unions naturally leads into a discussion of the remaining manner in which political objectives can be pursued in a democratic system, namely via the aggregation of particular interests as expressed through trade-union organizations. When the aggregate interests are the expression of a category as vast as the one formed by the workers, the organization or organizations which represent them have a greater political influence than that excercised by associations representing less important categories. But now we are being forced to recognize daily how great the impact of even tiny groups can be, groups which are in a position to paralyse a crucial sector of national life, such as transport. Naturally, these various forms of aggregating interests constitute an indirect way of exerting political influence within the parameters of the system. The thesis that the protagonist of the transformation of the capitalist system is not the party but the union is an old idea of revolutionary syndicalism which the New Left has never seriously revived, and was in any case never in a position to revive in a historical situation where the trade union had become a player provided for and to some extent regulated by the system itself. What is more, all the various schools of the revolutionary Left had been directly influenced by Leninism, which had made the vanguard party and not the union the agent of transformation (a transformation which presupposed that the seizure of power would be carried out by the self-same vanguard party).

The subject of political activism in a democratic society would not be exhausted if we did not take into account the mobilization of interests which are not specifically economic but relate to the conditions which promote such things as the development of the personality, covered by the useful, but cryptic, modern phrase the 'quality of life'. I am referring both to social movements such as the women's movement, various youth movements, the gay liberation movement, and to movements of public opinion which set out to defend and promote fundamental rights, such as the various leagues for human rights, or for defending linguistic or racial minorities, such as Amnesty International, which has among other things launched a campaign to abolish capital punishment throughout the world. A democratic system recognizes these movements and, within limits which vary from country to country, tolerates them, on the basis of the two fundamental principles of freedom of association and freedom of opinion. These two principles are to be interpreted as the essential preconditions for the proper working of the rules of the game, particularly for the most basic rule defining democracy, which establishes that no collective decision taken is binding or can be put into effect unless its legality in the last analysis depends on a consensus which has expressed itself via the exercise of universal suffrage in periodic elections. Freedom of association and freedom of opinion are to be regarded as preconditions for the proper functioning of a democratic system, because, as befits a system based on responding to demands expressed from below, and on the free choice of which policies to adopt or which delegates are to decide, it puts the representatives in a position to formulate their own demands and to take decisions after due consideration and free debate. Naturally neither freedom of association nor freedom of opinion can be completely unrestricted, which is true of any freedom. The shift in the limits one way or another determines the degree of democracy enjoyed in a system. Where the limits are extended the democratic system undergoes modification, where the two freedoms are suppressed democracy ceases to exist altogether.

It goes without saying that even political agitation by social movements or pressure groups, precisely because it is tolerated by the system and forms an integral part of the rules of the game, cannot result in the transformation of the system, at least as long as the system has the power to control it or limit it without eradicating it altogether. What has been happening in Italy is a prime example of the problems of distinguishing legitimate from illegitimate forms of association, admissible from inadmissible opinions. But the basic criterion which allows them to be distinguished is always in the last resort the safeguarding of the system as a whole, meaning by 'system' what has been defined above as an integral complex of rules, players and a code of conduct.

I do not know whether the reflections I have been formulating here can be considered overall to be reasonable and realistic. I know for a fact that they will be considered disillusioning and discouraging by those who, faced with the degradation of public life in Italy, the shameful spectacle of corruption, of sheer ignorance, careerism and cynicism which the bulk of our professional politicans present us with every day (there are exceptions but not enough to change the general picture), think that the channels of political activity allowed by the system are inadequate to bring about reforms, let alone radically transform it, and that extreme evils call for extreme remedies (but there are extreme remedies, such as terrorism, which only have the effect of making the evils worse). People who think in these terms feel constrained by acceptance of the rules of the system and forced to suffer from an acute sense of impotence, which they seek to overcome by refusing to resign themselves to the role of passive spectators, with the loss of so many hopes this implies.

The present writer belongs to a generation of people who lost their hopes more than thirty years ago, shortly after the end of the war, and have never recovered them except for occasional moments, as rare as they were fleeting, and which came to nothing. They came at the rate of one per decade: the revocation of the 'Legge Truffa' (1953),[9] the formation of the Centre-Left bloc (1964),[10] the great revival of the Communist Party (1975).[11] If I wanted to find some sort of pattern in the three events which inspired such optimism the first could be interpreted as the end of a regressive development within democracy, the second as the realignment of the dominant party away from alliances with the Right (excluding the extreme right Movimento Socialista Italiano or MSI)[12] towards accommodation with the Left, the third as the heralding of an effective alternative Left. As someone who has been through many years of frustrated hopes, I have learnt to be resigned to my own impotence. I am all the more resigned because, having lived half my life (the formative years) under Fascism, I stubbornly persist in my belief, like most of my contemporaries by the way, that a bad democracy (and Italy's is really bad) is still preferable to a good dictatorship (as a dictatorship Mussolini's was certainly better than Hitler's). It is better to have no foreign policy at all than one which is aggressive, warmongering and doomed to catastrophe. To have ten bickering parties is better than having one 'monolithically' united under the infallible leadership of its *duce*. A corporate society which retains its liberty is less intolerable than the corporate state and so on. But I fully accept that these arguments carry no weight with the young in Italy, who have not known Fascism and know only this democracy of ours, which is less than mediocre, and so are not equally disposed to accept the argument of the lesser evil. On the contrary, this younger generation has been through the events of 1968, which were so exhilirating even if they did come to naught, and ever since then it cannot reconcile itself to the party being over, expecially when faced with an everyday reality which is not just banal but, it is sad to say, tragic as well. It might be possible to explain why this heady period turned out to be a non-event: it was on the surface a momentous movement affecting universities, schools, and some factories, in major cities. But how deep did it go and what about the rest of the country? At bottom what change took place in the real society, which cannot be seen because it does not appear on the front page of the newspapers, in the society of the 'silent majority' who continued to vote for the Christian Democrats as if nothing had happened, or who gave a few more votes to the Communists in 1975 and 1976, and then partly withdrew these votes, or who spent most of their free time discussing league football matches, or reading, and still read, comics and magazines? Had it changed? Or had it stayed the same? And if it was slowly changing, was it really because society as a whole was imperceptibly changing, and not because a handful of hot-headed youths inspired by a sincere sense of justice had unfurled the flag of struggle against inequality, repression, consumerism and privilege, wanting to install imagination rather than obtuseness in power?[13]

The argument of the lesser evil is, I realise, meagre consolation. And there is not much comfort either in the argument that changes in society are almost always slow, almost invisible, and that it is important not to be too impatient. This second point cannot console the young for their inability to modify the present state of affairs, by comparison with which the years when the student revolts broke out can now be seen as years of prosperity and political and human relations which were still decent (the degeneration of our political system in Italy must be traced back to the right-wing terrorist outrage in the Piazza Fontana).[14] But it can explain why the sense of impotence gave way to the so-called *riflusso*, to an 'ebb' in political activism.[15]

The fact that the *riflusso* has become a catch-all for quite distinct forms of 'new quietism' has already been commented on elsewhere.[16] Thus it seems worthwhile to attempt a taxonomic description of this phenomenon, especially because it seems the only way to begin to see whether the trend could be reversed. A taxonomy of the 'new quietism' involves discerning within the general phenomenon the presence of distinct elements which call for distinct remedies (assuming they are to be treated like diseases to be cured). I believe it is possible to identify three which for want of anything better I will call the withdrawal from politics, the renunciation of politics and the rejection of politics.

The first is best summed up in the maxim: 'politics is not everything.' An expression which is the total antithesis of the belief in the omnipresence of politics, which was one of the major themes of the theory and practice of the student-power generation of the 1960s. At the end of the day, I do not believe that the new principle (which is actually as old as the hills) is at all regressive, and even less is it reactionary or cynical. The wholesale politicization of personal life is a road that leads to the total state and to what Dahrendorf has called the total citizen, for whom the *polis* is everything and the individual is nothing. We are direct heirs of a historical tradition in which the state is not everything and in every age there has always existed alongside the state a 'non-state' in the form of a religious community separate from the political community, or of a *vita contemplativa* in contrast with the *vita activa*, if only in the sense of economic relations confined within the family unit or opening onto the local market, which were distinct from the relations of sheer domination which characterize the state. Only in exceptional moments of rapid and profound transformation can political activities absorb all energies and become predominant and exclusive, a time when the demarcation between public and private evaporates and thoughts of leisure are banished. But these moments are short-lived, as was my generation's involvement in the Resistance against Fascism (at the end of which many went back to their normal jobs, which they had interrupted but never cancelled from their mind). In the moments when political action returns to its proper sphere where the passion for power reigns supreme and demands the skills of the lion and the fox, the ordinary citizen takes refuge in private life, now extolled as the port which offers shelter from the tempests of history. Of such times the philosopher writes: 'These disorders, however, do not move me to laughter nor even to tears, but rather to philosophizing and to the better observation of human nature . . . But now I let every man live according to his own ideas. Let those who will, by all means die for their good, so long as I am allowed to live for the truth.'[17] The Epicureans preach abstension from political life at the time of the crisis of the Greek cities, the Libertines in the age when the wars of religion were raging. The last few years have witnessed a renewed celebration of the primacy of spiritual life, or of moral principles over simple politics, with a fervour which has not been seen in our culture for decades. This trend can be seen in Soviet dissidents such as Solzhenitsyn and Zinoviev (to quote two writers who are culturally at opposite poles to each other). Down the centuries the exhortation to 'render unto Caesar the things that are Caesar's, and to God the things which are God's' has remained constant. The inability to tell the two spheres apart, the exclusive concentration of energy on one sphere alone, is the mark of the fanatic (and only in rare cases of the genius). On the contrary, the lives of ordinary people are lived out in most cases in areas which lie outside the one occupied by politics and which politics crowds in on but never invades entirely. When it does take them over it is a sign that the individual has been reduced to a cog in car engine and has no clear idea of who the driver is and where he is driving.

The second attitude, that of renunciation, can be summed up in another maxim: 'Politics is not for everyone.'[18] The difference between the two approaches is clear enough and requires no special comment. The first concerns the limits of political activity, the second the limits to which people are called upon to participate in this activity. It is possible to imagine a situation where politics is everything but not for everyone, as in a totalitarian state, or at the other extreme, a situation where politics is not everything but is for everyone, corresponding to a state which is both democratic and liberal. Between these two extremes there is the situation where politics is not everything and is not for all, as exemplified by the oligarchical state of the past (and even if camouflaged under an assumed name, in modern democracies). Finally there is the one where politics is everything and for everyone, for which it is only possible to give a hypothetical model never realized and perhaps (I would add fortunately) unrealizable, namely the republic conceived by Rousseau in his *Social Contract*[19] (this approximates closest to the model which the Italian student power movement of '68 had more or less in mind, apart from the small nuclei of neo-Marxist-Leninists or Stalinists of the old guard).

Both maxims can be interpreted as simple statements of fact, i.e. observations which all of us can acknowledge without getting too worked up, impartially, as neutral onlookers. But they can also be taken as proposing a course of action or necessary reform, as if one were saying that everything is politics, it is true, but it would be better if it were not, or that politics is now for everyone but it would be preferable if not everybody interfered in things that do not concern them, or in which they have no expertise. The basic point is, therefore, that the statement 'not everything is political' can be taken to mean two different things:

(a)   history shows that politics is only one of the basic human activities;
(b)   an advanced society is one where politics does not invade the whole of human life.

In the same way the statement 'politics is not for everyone' can mean:

(a)   it is an incontrovertible historical fact that active politics is only ever the province of a small minority, even in so-called democratic societies;
(b)   an advanced society is one where there is a certain division of labour, so that the majority of citizens are relieved of the daily duty to be actively involved in public affairs.

In the past there have been at least two significant versions of the second maxim taken as a statement of fact: one conservative, the theory of elites, one revolutionary, the theory of the vanguard party. But irrespective of theories, which are often laden with ideological presuppositions (and are, as Pareto would have said, pseudo-scientific theories, or simply 'derivations')[20] even the man or woman in the street cannot help noticing the '*palazzo*', or town hall, where a few gain access to the doors marked 'private' or are invited to the banquets, and the others, if they are lucky, stand around and watch. In fact everything about this *palazzo* turns out to be partially invisible, like the castle in a fairy-tale. Then again, taking the maxim positively, i.e. as the prescription of a positive mode of behaviour, it is the sentiment characteristic of a disdainful attitude towards the masses, the plebs, the rabble, which has been typical of oligarchies as long as they have existed. Nowadays it is also typical of technocratic circles, for whom the dichotomy is no longer between the wise and the stupid, but between the competent and the incompetent (where the criterion for telling them apart is no longer the possession of wisdom but of scientific knowledge). Finally, there is a way of interpreting the two maxims prescriptively as rejections of an undesirable state of affairs: in fact politics is not all-pervasive but it would be good if it were, or it is true that not everyone is politically involved but an ideal society is one where all are citizens on equal footing and with an equal degree of political commitment. As statements of what is to be condemned such maxims are typical of the democratic creed, of the faith in popular participation, of the celebration of power from below as opposed to hierarchical power, of autonomy contrasted with heteronomy, of the conviction that everyone is the best judge of his own interests, of the rejection of any form of delegated authority.

The third attitude which I have called the rejection of politics, is more exclusive than the first two and perhaps because of its radicalism is the one that best characterizes the phenomenon of the 'new quietism'. I have just said that the first two can also be interpreted as statements of fact. The third, however, always implies a value-judgement on politics. In the case of this attitude the distinction to be drawn, if any, so as to complete this rapid taxonomic survey, is between two different ways, one crude the other more noble, of condemning politics. The first, predominantly egoistic and particularist, is typical of the petit-bourgeois attachment to social and material self-interest, known in Italian as *qualunquismo*, [21] and which conforms to the principle that the wise person literally minds his own business, and if someone gets involved in politics it can only be for motives of personal gain. Hence there are no ideals, and ideals bandied about are lies. Human beings only do something when motivated by vested interests, which vary in size according to people's circumstances and ambitions, so that everyone should look after his own interests, protecting them from the so-called public interest, which is always the private interest of the few. The other attitude, based on religious ethics and always an

undercurrent of the Western philosophical tradition, is characteristic of someone who is unable to see in politics anything other than
the 'demonic face of power' (far more tragic than the face of the
charlatan, which alienates the cynical *qualunquisti),* and considers
politics to be the sphere where what dominates unchallenged is the
will to power, which works specifically to the advantage of the
strongest. In this sphere the only recognized way of resolving
conflicts is violence, and history the only tribunal to judge right and
wrong since it has always upheld the rights of the victor, so that ideals
are nothing but a way of taking the credulous masses when the only
thing at stake is to win power, and once this has been achieved the
ideals are systematically betrayed. Perhaps the first of these two
attitudes is too myopic, while the second errs in being excessively
long-sighted. The first gives rise to the concept of a society which can
survive with a state apparatus reduced to the minimum, and which
has no other concern than to make sure that each is enabled to
pursue as freely as possible his or her own private interests. The
other leads to the ideal of the society of scholars, the republic of
sages or of philosophers, of a state which becomes a church, of the
reign of the sophisticated, in which moral laws voluntarily respected
totally replace juridic laws imposed by force. Two Utopias, if you
like, but which correspond so well to real and continually recurring
states of mind that we cannot avoid taking them seriously if for no
other reason than that they reveal a permanent dissatisfaction with
political reality, a dissatisfaction which wells up at times in all of us
with an intensity which varies according to our moods and our
circumstances.

Of course this taxonomy of the *riflusso* may explain a lot and make
it appear more ordinary than it must seem to those who, for a brief
phase of their lives, believed sincerely in total commitment. But it
offers no way out to someone who adopts an attitude of detachment,
renunciation or rejection, not towards politics in general, but
towards *politics in Italy,* and believes that over and above the
traditional avenues of political action, in respect of which the different positions just described may even be valid, there is an alternative
form of politics, that politics transcends its negative aspects and
acquires positive value when it is conceived as an activity not
directed to self-interest but to the common good, not only to living,
but, as Aristotle claimed, to living well.

But where are these ways out? In the questionnaire that we have
been given to fill out,[22] there is an allusion near the end to new forms
of 'political practice', such as civil disobedience, self-determination
and the exercise of the veto. To make them sound more impressive

they are presented as 'rights', and in fact there is talk of the 'right to civil disobedience', 'the right to self-determination' and the 'right of veto'. But are we really dealing with rights? Only in the case of self-determination is it strictly speaking possible to talk of a right, that is if it is understood as a form of right of association under Article 18 of the Constitution. However, the principle of association can be used to stir the waters but not to unleash the tempest. As for the right to civil disobedience, this simply does not exist. Quite the reverse, for Article 54 lays down the opposite duty, namely to 'observe the Constitution and the laws'. The same must be said of the right of veto, if it is taken literally to mean the right to block a collective decision with a solitary vote against the motion, because in a democratic system the sovereign rule is that of the majority decision and not of unanimity.[23] This is not to deny that both civil disobedience and the veto can be used in specific circumstances as specific forms of *de facto* power. In the case of civil disobedience, for example, one could cite a situation where the number of people who refuse to comply with an order issued by the authorities, or for that matter a parliamentary law, is so great that it makes repression practically impossible. As for the veto, it can happen that a single vote or the vote of a single group is decisive in forming a majority, something that happens publicly every day in Italy in the coalitions of the Christian Democrats with minor parties, which hold the balance of power needed to convert a relative majority into an absolute one.[24] But, precisely because *de facto* powers are involved such tactics require either extreme force or particularly favourable exceptional circumstances to be effective. They are not like rights which can be invoked on every occasion they are deemed to have been violated. Presenting them as if they were rights is misleading, because it implies that they are, like all other rights, guaranteed; whereas this is precisely what they are not, and anyone relying on the notion that they are runs the risk of landing up in prison. It is not only misleading but dangerous, because it could divert energies, indispensable for the political struggles already taking place, towards misconceived and impracticable solutions. Doubtless legal relations can be modified in the wake of modifications in power relations. But precisely for this reason it is vital to realize that we are dealing with power relations and not with an appeal to guaranteed rights, and that to change the balance of power it is essential, as Signor de la Palisse[25] would have said, to have the necessary force. I am not prepared to discuss whether the necessary force exists, though personally I am sceptical. I am simply saying that it is mistaken to confuse a series of events, or rather the desire for certain events to take place, with a right.

To sum up: I have already stated that, staying within the parameters provided by the rules of the game, the possible routes are as they are, and that the steps taken along them are predictable, almost predetermined. Moreover, even assuming it is easy to depart from the rules of the game (and we have seen that it is not), I do not believe this to be desirable, because once the most fundamental of these rules, the one that provides for periodic elections, is broken, no one can know where it will lead to. Personally I believe it would lead to disaster. This is not the place to go over old ground, but what gave birth to the working-class movement was the idea that democracy was a bourgeois institution and that it was necessary to adopt an alternative form of politics. Then gradually the movement not only secured representative democracy, but through universal suffrage actually consolidated it. Within this representative democracy I can see no other solution for Italy in the foreseeable future than the one offered by the Left (which is not the nebulous 'democratic alternative' the Communists refer to). Everything else is something in between castles in the air and agitation for agitation's sake, which in the short or long term is liable only to aggravate frustrations. But even this little is so uncertain that to look for anything else means embarking once again on a road full of expectations doomed to disappointment.

# 4

# Democracy and Invisible Power

A few years ago I published some reflections on the 'paradoxes' of democracy, namely the objective difficulties encountered by any attempt to find a correct application of democratic principles in those very societies where there are increasing calls for the extension of democracy.[1] Among those who consider democracy to be the ideal of 'good government' (in the classic sense of the word, i.e. in the sense of a government that succeeds better than any other in realizing the common good), the other topic which is continually being debated concerns what might be called the 'failures' of democracy. Much of what is written about democracy nowadays boils down to a denunciation, sometimes heartbroken sometimes triumphant in tone, of these failures. The now classic issue of elitism falls under this heading, as does the even more classic one of the gulf between formal and substantive democracy. The controversy which has surfaced in recent years over the 'ungovernability' of society could also be included. However I feel that political commentators have still not given one issue the attention which it deserves: this is the question of 'invisible power'. What follows is a preliminary attempt to chart this unmapped area.

### THE PUBLIC RULE OF PUBLIC POWER

One of the clichés heard in all past and present debates on democracy is the assertion that it is 'open government' by a 'visible power'. Almost every day you can come across platitudes to the effect that it is in the 'nature of democracy' for 'nothing to stay relegated to the realm of mystery'.[2] Making a play on words, we might define the rule of democracy as the rule of public power in public. The pun is only apparent, because 'public' has two meanings depending on whether it is used as the opposite of 'private', as in the classic distinction between *ius publicum* and *ius privatum*, bequeathed to us by Roman jurists, or of 'secret', in which case it does not mean pertaining to the *res publica* i.e. 'public thing' or state, but denotes 'manifest', 'obvious', i.e. 'visible'. Precisely because the two meanings do not overlap, a public spectacle may very well be a private affair, and a private school (in the sense that it does not belong to the state) cannot avoid public scrutiny of its acts. Thus, in the light of the distinction between private and public law, the private character of the power exercised by the head of a family is not in the least infringed by the public accountability of many of the acts performed in that role, and equally the total secrecy in which autocratic rulers wields their power does not in the least alter the fact that his power is of a public character.

The idea of democracy as a political system based on visible power immediately evokes the image, handed down to us by political writers of all epochs who have invoked the illustrious example of Pericles' Athens, of the *agora*, or of the *ecclesia*, in other words the congregation of all the citizens in a public place for the purpose of formulating and hearing proposals, denouncing abuses, making accusations, and, having heard the arguments for and against expounded by the orators, reaching decisions either with a show of hands or by a ballot using pieces of pottery. When the citizens had assembled, writes Glotz, the herald solemnly cursed anyone who might seek to deceive the people, and so that the demagogues would not abuse their rhetorical skills the assembly remained permanently under the 'watchful eye' of God (note this reference to the act of 'seeing'). Magistrates were subjected to continual supervision, and 'nine times a year at every prytaneum they were obliged to have their powers renewed in a vote of confidence carried out with a show of hands, and if they did not secure this they were automatically summoned before the tribunal.'[3] It is not for nothing that the assembly has often been compared with a theatre or stadium, that is to say a public spectacle in which there are indeed spectators, called upon to witness a series of actions staged according to rules agreed in advance and which finishes with a judgement. In a passage of *The Laws* in which Plato is talking of a time when people were subject to laws and quotes the example of the respect for the laws of music, he recounts how gradually, thanks to works by poets swept away by 'a Dionysian rapture', a deplorable confusion between various musical styles had come about and a neglect of the laws of music had been engendered in the common people, with the result that 'our once silent audiences have found a voice, in the persuasion that they understand what is good and bad in art; and instead of there being an aristocracy in music we now have a miserable theatrocracy.'[4] He goes on immediately to redefine this newly coined term 'theatrocracy' as 'democracy in matters of music', interpreting it as the result of the claim of the common peole to be qualified to talk about everything without acknowledging any longer the existence of laws. Plato is an anti-democratic writer. The equation of rule of the people and the rule of the public in a theatre (with the resulting distinction between rule of the public and rule of the best) enables him to express yet again his own condemnation of democracy, interpreted by him as the reign of licence and lawlessness. But the comparison of the *demos* with a theatre audience has implications which go far beyond the value judgement given it in the extract from Plato.[5]

The evocative power conveyed by the concept of classical democracy during the age of the French Revolution is well known. It is irrelevant in this context if the actual reality had ever conformed to the model or whether in the course of centuries it simply became transformed into a normative ideal. The fact is that democratic government continued to be throughout this period, and even more intensely in moments when crises or expectations of a *novus ordo* came to a head, the ideal model of public rule exercised in public. Of the countless works produced in the revolutionary period, I cite this exemplary passage from *Catechismo repubblicano* by Michele Natale (the bishop of Vico, eventually executed in Naples on 20 August 1799):

> Is there nothing secret in Democratic Government? All the activities of those in power must be known to the Sovereign People, except for some measures of public security, details of which must be divulged once the danger has ceased.[6]

This quotation is exemplary because in a few phrases it articulates one of the fundamental principles of the constitutional state: publicity (in its original sense of being open to public scrutiny) is the rule, secrecy the exception, and it is an exception that should not violate the rule since secrecy is justified, just like all other exceptional measures (such as those the Roman dictator could take) even if it is for a limited period only.[7]

It has always been regarded as one of the cardinal principles of the democratic system that all the decisions and, generally speaking, the activities of those in power must be known to the sovereign people defined as direct government by the people or government controlled by the people (and how could it be controlled if it was kept secret?) Even when the ideal of direct democracy was abandoned as an anachronism with the emergence of the large modern territorial state (and the small territorial state had also long since ceased to be a city-state) and replaced by the ideal of representative democracy, the principles of which are already clearly expounded in a letter from Madison to his critics as part of a debate whose subject is precisely classical democracy,[8] nevertheless the public character of power, understood as not secret, as open to the 'public', remained one of the fundamental criteria to distinguish the constitutional state from the absolute state, and hence indicated the birth (or rebirth) of public power in public. In a section of his *Verfassungslehre*, Carl Schmitt expresses very well, even if unintentionally and in a very different context to this, the intimate connection between representation and the 'publicity' of power, and goes so far as to take representation in its literal sense of presenting, making present or visible, what otherwise would stay hidden. It is worth quoting two passages at least:

> Representation can only proceed in the in the public sphere. There is no representation which takes place in secret or *in camera* ... A parliament only has a representative character as long as it is believed that its proper activity is a public affair. Secret sessions, secret agreements and consultations of some committee or other can be very significant and important, but they can never have a representative character.[9]

The second passage is even more explicit in the bearing it has on the subject.

> To represent means to make visible and present an invisible entity through an entity which is publicly present. The dialectic of the concept lies in the fact that the invisible is assumed to be absent but simultaneously made present.[10]

As well as the problem of representation, there is another related but separate issue which has grown up as part of democratic theory and which is also intimately bound up with the question of invisible power: that of decentralization, by which is meant a revaluation of the political relevance of the periphery with respect to the centre of power. The ideal of local government can be interpreted as an ideal inspired by the principle that the closer power is physically, the more visible it is. In fact its visibility does not not depend solely on the fact that the person who is invested with power presents himself publicly, but also on the spatial proximity between the rulers and the ruled. Even if mass communications have shortened the distance between the person who is, or is to be, elected and the electors, the publicity of national parliament is indirect, being largely effected via the press, and the publication of parliamentary proceedings, of laws and other deliberations in the equivalent of the Italian Gazetta Ufficiale or the British Hansard. In a local authority the publicity of government is more direct, and is more direct because the administrators and their deliberations are more accessible to the public. Or at least one of the arguments always used by defenders of local government, the argument for the limitation of the scale of centres of power and their proliferation, has been that it offers citizens more possibilities to keep an eye personally on the issues that concern them and to leave as little room as possible for invisible power.

Some years ago, in a book that was widely known and discussed, Habermas traced the history of the transformation of the modern state by showing the gradual emergence of what he termed 'the private sphere of the public'. By this he meant the growing social relevance both of the private sphere and of the sphere of so-called public opinion, which claims the right to discuss and criticize the actions of public authorities and hence demands, as it could not fail to do, the publicity of debates, judicial debates just as much as strictly political debates.[11] It goes without saying that the degree of relevance of public opinion (in the sense of opinion relating to public acts, i.e. acts pertaining to the public's political power *par excellence*, namely the power exercised by the supreme decision-making institutions of the state, of the '*res publica*') depends on the degree to which the acts of whoever holds supreme power are made available for public scrutiny, meaning how far they are visible, ascertainable, accessible, and hence accountable. Understood in this sense, publicity is a typical Enlightenment concept in that it perfectly embodies one of the battle-fronts of those who consider themselves called to defeat the realm of darkness. Whatever sphere it spread to, the metaphor of light and enlightenment (of *Aufklärung* and *illuminismo*) expresses well the contrast between visible and invisible power. In a section on the 'solar myth of the revolution' Starobinski reminds the reader that Fichte, enthusiastic supporter of the French Revolution, had dated from Heliopolis, 'the last year of the obscurantism of the past', his discourse on the *Demand for the Restitution by the Princes of Europe of the Freedom of Thought Which They Have Till Now Suppressed.*[13]

The thinker who, more than any other, has contributed to clarifying the interrelationship between public opinion and the publicity of power is Kant, who can justly be considered the starting point of every discussion on the necessity for power to be visible, a necessity which is for him not only political but moral. In his famous essay on Enlightenment, Kant maintains adamantly that it lays claims to 'the most innocuous of all freedoms – freedom to make *public* use of one's reason in all matters'. He follows this assertion with the comment: 'The *public* use of man's reason must always be free, and it alone can bring about enlightenment among men', where by 'public use of one's own reason' is meant 'that use which anyone may make of it *as a man of learning* addressing the entire *reading public*.' As is well known, this comment accompanies a eulogy of Frederick II who had encouraged religious freedom and freedom of thought, the latter being understood as the authorisation of his subjects 'to use their own reason' and 'publicly submit to the judgement of the world their verdicts and opinions, even if they deviate here and there from orthodox doctrine'.[14] Naturally the public use of reason necessitates the publicity of the acts of the sovereign. Kant's thought is quite explicit on this point and deserves more attention, not least for its topicality today, than even his most perceptive critics have hitherto given it. In the second Appendix to his *Perpetual Peace*, entitled 'On the Agreement between Politics and Morality according to the Transcendental Concept of Public Right', Kant considers as the 'transcendental concept of public right' the following principle: 'All actions affecting the rights of other human beings are wrong if their maxim is not compatible with their being made public.'[15] What does this principle mean? In general terms a precept not susceptible to being publicized can be taken to mean a precept which, if it was ever made known to the public, would arouse such a public reaction that one could not put it into action. The applications Kant makes of this principle, using two illuminating examples relating to domestic and international law, illustrate the problem better than any further comment. With regard to domestic law he cites the example of the right of resistance, and for international law the right of the sovereign to violate pacts made with other sovereigns. His reasoning is as follows. In the first example he gives, 'the injustice of rebellion is thus apparent from the fact that if the maxim upon which it would act *were publicly acknowledged*, it would defeat its own purpose. This maxim would therefore have to be kept secret.'[16] Indeed, what citizen could publicly declare at the very moment of accepting the *pactum subiectionis*, that they reserve the right not to observe it? And what would such a pact be worth if it recognized that those who sign it have the right to break it? Similarly, to cite his second example, what would happen if in the very act of agreeing on the terms of a treaty with another state, one of the contracting states publicly declared that it did not consider itself bound by the obligations which arose from the agreement? Kant replies 'that everyone else would naturally flee from him, or unite with others in order to resist his pretensions; which proves that such a system of politics, for all its cunning, would defeat its own purpose if operated on a public footing, so that the above maxim must be wrong'.[17]

I do not think I need to stress the validity of this principle as a criterion for distinguishing good from bad government. Reading the newspapers which every morning provide further installments of public scandals (and Italy has the unenviable reputation of having a record number of such scandals), all of us can add any number of examples which corroborate the soundness of this principle. What does a public scandal consist of? Or, put another way, what arouses a public sense of scandal? And in what moment does a scandal occur? The moment in which a scandal occurs is the moment in which an act or a series of acts are disclosed to the public which had previously been kept secret or hidden, but only in so far that they could not be disclosed because, if they had been, that act or series of acts could not have been performed. Just think of the various forms that public corruption can take: embezzlement, misappropriation of funds, extortion, abuse of official authority for private gain—and these are banal examples, things that happen every day. What public official could declare in public the moment he assumes his official responsibilities that he will divert public funds into his own pockets (embezzlement), or purloin money not belonging to the public administration but which is in his possession because of his official duties (misappropriation of funds), or will force someone to give him money by misusing his powers or position (extortion) or will take advantage of his authority for personal gain (abuse of official powers)? It is obvious that any declarations of this sort would make it impossible for the intention to be carried out, because no public administration would entrust a responsible position to someone who behaved like this. This is the reason why actions of the sort must be performed in secret, and once divulged provoke a public outcry, which is precisely what has come to be known as 'scandal'. Only Plato's tyrant could carry out publicly even those heinous deeds which the private citizens either perform without anyone else knowing, or, if they have repressed the impulse, is reduced to performing only in his dreams, such as matricide. The criterion of publicity in order to distinguish what is just from what is unjust, the licit from the illicit, does not apply to people like tyrants, for whom public and private coincide in the sense that the affairs of state are their personal affair and vice versa.[18]

## AUTOCRACY AND 'ARCANA IMPERII'

The importance attached to the publicity of power is one aspect of the Enlightenment's polemic against the absolute state, or more specifically, against the various images of the paternalistic or authoritarian sovereign, of the monarch by divine right, or of the God on earth conceived by Hobbes. The father who imposes his will on his under-age sons, the slave-owner who gives orders to those subject to his command, the monarch who receives from God the right to rule, the sovereign who is compared to a God on earth, are under no obligation to disclose to those who receive their orders, who do not constitute a 'public', the secret whys and wherefores of their decisions. Tasso has Torrismondo say: '*I segreti de' regi al folle volgo/ ben commessi non sono*' ('It behoves not kings to confide their secrets to the foolish populace').[19] Following the principle '*salus rei publicae suprema lex*', the sovereigns by divine right, or by natural law, or by right of conquest, actually have the duty to keep their plans concealed as far as possible. Made in the image and likeness of the hidden God, the more successful the sovereigns are in seeing what their uncouth and recalcitrant subjects are doing without being seen themselves, the more powerful they will be, and hence the better they will perform their function of governing them. The ideal of the sovereign who is compared to God on earth is to be, like God, all-seeing and invisible. The political relationship, i.e. the relationship between ruler and ruled, can in this case be conceived as one of reciprocal exchange, or as the jurist would say a synallagmatic one, in which the ruler offers protection in return for obedience. Now those who protects need to be endowed with a thousand eyes like the eyes of Argos, while those who obey have no need to see anything whatsoever. The more farsighted the protection, the more blind the obedience.

One of the recurrent themes to be found in the theoretical writings on the *raison d'état*, which form a background to the formation of the modern state, is that of the *arcana imperii*. We are dealing with an enormous subject and I will thus limit myself to a few brief remarks which have a direct bearing on the matter in hand.[20] The author of the most celebrated work on the matter, *De arcanis rerum publicarum*, Clapmar, defines the *arcana imperii* as follows: '*Intimae et occultae rationes sive consilia eorum qui in republica principatum obtinent*', (The secret and hidden deliberations or resolutions of those who hold power in the state'.) Their purpose is twofold: to conserve the state as such and conserve the existing form of government (in other words prevent a monarchy from degenerating into an aristocracy, an aristocracy into a democracy, and so forth, following the natural course of the various 'mutations' illustrated by Aristotle in the fifth book of his *Politics*). The author calls the first '*arcana imperii*', the second '*arcana dominationis*'. [21] Both of them belong to the category of '*simulationes*', even if they are '*honestae et licitae*'. The Machiavellian Gabriel Naudé, in his *Considérations politiques sur les coups d'État*, writes: 'There is no prince so weak and devoid of sense that he is asinine to the point of submitting to public scrutiny something which will hardly remain secret if confided to the ear of a minister or favourite.'[22] From these quotations it is already clear that the category *arcana* includes two phenomena which are distinct even if they are intimately connected: the phenomenon of occult power, or power that *conceals itself*, and power which *conceals*, or hides itself by hiding something else. Subsumed in the first type is the classic question of the state secret, in the second the equally classic one of the 'noble', i.e. legitimate and useful lie (legitimate because useful) which goes back to none other than Plato. In the autocratic state the state secret is not the exception but the rule: important decisions must be taken away from the prying eyes of the public in any shape or form. The highest grade of public power, namely the power to make decisions binding for all subjects, coincides with the maximum degree of privacy surrounding rulers and their decisions. In a text that has come to be considered one of the most authoritative sources for the reconstruction of French political thought in the era of absolute monarchy, *La monarchie de France* by Claude de Seyssel, we read that 'it is also necessary to take heed not to communicate those things which are required to remain secret before too large a gathering. For it is almost impossible for what comes to the attention of several people not to become public knowledge.'[23] The king, according to this writer, needs to avail himself of three councils, just as Christ could count on three circles of followers, the seventy-two disciples, the twelve apostles, and the three most trustworthy companions, Saint Peter, Saint John and Saint Jacob. Of these three councils the inner sanctum is the Secret Council, composed of not more than three or four persons selected from 'the most wise and experienced', with whom heads of state settle major issues before raising them with the Ordinary Council. They will question the latter council's decision if they feel it was not the most appropriate one to have reached, even to the point of not acting on it and carrying out the decision of the Secret Council instead 'without telling them anything till it has already been put into effect'.[24] Among the reasons which can be invoked in favour of secrecy, the two prevalent ones are also the most frequently cited:

the necessity for all decisions concerning the supreme interests of the state to be expedited as quickly as possible, and disdain for the common people, who are considered a passive object of power, dominated as they are by strong passions which prevent them from forming a rational idea of the common good and which make them an easy prey for demagogues. It goes without saying that when I refer to the occult power of the autocrat I am not thinking of its external aspect. The more absolute rulers are, the more they must present themselves to the outside world with incontrovertible signs of their power: the royal palace in the centre of the city, the crown, sceptre and other regal insignia, the magnificence of the apparel, the retinue of nobles, the escort of armed men, the parade of symbols which are, in the true sense of the term, 'ostentatious', the arches of triumph along their route, the solemn ceremonies to make a public ritual out of the major moments of their private lives – weddings, births, deaths (all in marked contrast with the secrecy of their public acts). The brilliant, almost blinding, visibility of the actor, necessary to instil a sense of respect and reverential awe towards someone with the power of life and death over his own subjects, must be matched by the opaqueness of action necessary to guarantee that it will defy control or interference from outside.[25]

Conversely, where the supreme power is occult, power directed against it also tends to be occult. Invisible power and invisible opposition are two sides of the same coin. The history of every autocratic regime and the history of conspiracy run parallel to each other. Where there is secret power there exists, almost as its natural by-product, an equally secret 'anti-power' in the form of conspiracies, plots, cabals, *coups d'états*, hatched in the antechambers of the imperial palace, or else of seditious acts, revolts or rebellions planned in impenetrable, inaccessible places, far from the watchful eyes of the palace authorities, just as the ruler acts as much as possible out of sight of the common people. A history of the *arcana seditionis* could be written to be placed alongside the history of the *arcana dominationis* and with the same wealth of detail. The subject disappeared from the treatises on political science and public law only with the advent of the modern constitutional state which proclaimed the principle of the publicity of power. But the question was not neglected in the classics of political thought and it would not come amiss, for reasons all too obvious, and tragically so, to carefully peruse once more the relevant pages. In his *Discorsi sulla prima deca*, Machiavelli devotes one of his most densely argued and lengthy chapters to conspiracy and opens it with these words: 'Since conspiracies are of such dangerous consequences alike to princes and to private persons, I cannot well omit to discuss their nature, for it is plain that many more princes have lost their lives and their states in this way than by open war.' He goes on: 'Hence, in order that princes may learn how to guard against these dangers, and that private persons may think twice before undertaking them . . . I shall speak of conspiracies at length, omitting nothing of importance that is relevant to either a prince or to a private person.'[26]

Autocratic power, as I have said, not only conceals itself so as not to disclose where it is, but also tends to conceal its real intentions at the moment when its decisions have to be made public. Self-concealment as well as concealment are two of the customary strategies for ensuring power remains occult. When you cannot avoid mixing with the public you don a mask. For writers on the *raison détat* the subject of 'falsehood' is an obligatory theme, as is the invocation of the 'noble lie' of Plato or the 'sophistic discourses' of Aristotle.[27] It became a *communis opinio*, that whoever holds power and must continually be on the watchout for external and internal enemies, has the right to lie, or, to be precise, to 'simulate', i.e. make something appear to be the case when it is not, and to 'dissimulate', or make appear not to be the case what is. The comparison ritually invoked is that of the doctor who conceals from his patient the seriousness of an illness. But equally ritualistic is the condemnation of patients who deceive the doctor and, by not telling the truth about the gravity of their diseases, prevent him from effecting a cure. By analogy, while it is true that the prince has the right to deceive his subject, it is equally true that the subject has no right to deceive the prince. The great Bodin writes: 'There is no need to be sparing of either fine words or promises: indeed Plato and Xenophon allowed magistrates and rulers to lie, as adults do with babies and invalids. Thus the sage Pericles behaved with the Athenians to direct them onto the path of reason.'[28] Grotius dedicates a chapter of his *De iure belli ac pacis* to the subject *De dolis et mendacio* in international relations. This chapter is important because it includes a long list of classical opinions for and against public lies, as well as a sustained piece of casuistry, so sustained and subtle that modern readers lose their way in a labyrinth where at the end of one path new ones open up before them to the point where they find themselves going hopelessly astray, unable to find the way out or to turn back.

The highest ideal inspiring the type of power which is both all-seeing and invisible has recently been rediscovered and marvellously described by Foucault in his analysis of Bentham's design for the Panopticon: an arrangement of separate cells, each one enclosing a prisoner, radiating out from a centre where there stands a turret from the top of which the guardian, symbol of power, can at any moment observe even the slightest movements of those he keeps a watch on.[29] The important thing is not that the prisoners see the person who sees them: what matters is that they know that there is someone who sees them, or rather that he can see them. Foucault correctly defines the Panopticon as a machine for 'dissociating the see/be seen dyad'. With his scheme he who sees is not seen. He puts it in these words: 'In the peripheric ring, one is totally seen without ever seeing; in the central tower one sees everything without ever being seen.'[30] Another interesting observation: the architectural structure of the Panopticon establishes an essential asymmetry between the two parties in the power relationship centering on the act of seeing or of being seen. It is an observation which leads to a further insight: power relations can be both symmetrical and asymmetrical. Ideally the democratic form of government comes about via an agreement between each person with everyone else, i.e. with the *pactum societatis*. Now the contract represents the ideal-type of a symmetrical relationship, based as it is on the principle *do ut des*, while the ideal-type of the asymmetrical arrangement is the system where the sovereign establishes a relationship based on command and obedience. The structure of the Panopticon was invented as a model prison, in other words as a type of social institution based on the principle of maximum coercion and minimum freedom, a so-called total institution, like lunatic asylums, barracks, and to some extent hospitals, which operate on the precept that 'Everything which is not prohibited is obligatory.' But such a set-up can easily be exalted to become the ideal model of the autocratic state when its principle is taken to its logical conclusion (here I use the term 'principle' in Montesquieu's sense),[31] and leads to the axiom that the more the prince is all-seeing the more he is able to make himself obeyed, and the more he is invisible the more capable he is of commanding. If we take the pair command/obedience as the epitome of the asymmetrical power relationship, the more hidden from sight the person who commands, the more terrible he is (the subject knows that there is someone looking at him but does not know exactly where he is). By the same token, the more the person who has to obey is observable and is observed in every gesture, deed or word, the more docile he will be (the sovereign knows at any moment where he is and what he is doing).

It was also Bentham who glimpsed the possibility, as Foucault has admirably demonstrated, of extending the mechanism of the Panopticon to other institutions, to all establishments 'in which, within a space not too large to be covered or commanded by buildings, a number of persons are meant to be kept under inspection', because 'its great excellence consists in the great strength it is capable of giving to *any* institution it may be thought proper to apply it to.'[32] I will come back at the end to the phrase 'within a space which is not too large'. Worth stressing here are the Utopian heights which the inventor's infatuation with his creation reached: Bentham lists the benefits of the Panopticon in these terms: '*Morals reformed – health preserved – industry invigorated – instruction diffused – public burdens lightened* – Economy seated, as it were, on a rock – the Gordian knot of the Poor-laws not cut, but untied – all by a simple idea in architecture.'[33] The very shape of the building – above the warder on the tower keeping watch, below the prisoner in his cell being watched – raises a final question which is the one that political writers of all times, from Plato onwards, have posed at the end of every theory of the state: 'Who supervises the supervisor?' – '*Quis custodiet custodes?*' The ritual reply consists in postulating a hierarchy of supervisors till you necessarily (it being impossible in practical terms to invoke the principle of infinite regression) arrive at a supervisor who is unsupervised because there is no one of superior rank. But who is this unsupervised supervisor? The question is so important that the various political doctrines can be classified in terms of the reply they give to it: God, the heroic founder of states (Hegel), the strongest, the revolutionary party who has conquered power, the people conceived as the whole community which expresses its will by voting. Bentham is in his own way a democratic writer and this is how he resolves the problem of the supervised supervisor: the building can be easily submitted to continuous inspections not only by designated inspectors but by the public. This expedient represents a further phase in sundering the paired concept 'see/be seen'. The prisoner is seen but unseeing, the guard sees and is seen, the people closes the progression by seeing but remaining unseen by anyone but itself and hence, vis à vis others, is invisible. The unseen seer is once again sovereign.

### DEMOCRATIC IDEAL AND REALITY

The foregoing observations have shown, I believe, not only the importance but the vastness of a question which has, so far, been less thoroughly explored than it deserves. And I have not yet even mentioned a crucial phenomenon in the history of secret power, namely the phenomenon of espionage (and, correspondingly, since invisible power is combatted by another power which is equally invisible, of counter-espionage), and more generally the use of secret agents. There has never been a state, whether autocratic or democratic, which has done without them. And no state has so far done without them because there is no better way of knowing about other peoples activities than trying to obtain knowledge of them without being known or recognized. It is no coincidence if Kant, whose thesis concerning the publicity of acts of government as a remedy for the immorality of politics I have already highlighted, considers one of the preconditions of perpetual peace between states to be an absolute ban on the use of spies. He includes the resort to them among the 'dishonourable strategems', and one of the arguments he cites is that the deployment of spies in war, a strategem which 'exploits only the dishonesty of others', will eventually spread even to peacetime.[34]

It goes without saying – I was going to say it is an 'open secret' – that even the most democratic state guarantees citizens a sphere of privacy or secrecy, for example by making violation of private correspondence a crime (Article 616 C.P.)[35] or with legislation which protects the privacy and intimacy of individual or family life from the prying eyes of public authorities or the agencies in society which mould public opinion. For instance Articles 683-685 C.P.[36] (so often invoked whether appropriate or not) make it a crime to divulge secret parliamentary discussions, details of court proceedings or information relating to a trial in progress. But this is not the point: there is still a difference nonetheless between autocracy and democracy in that for the former the secrecy of state matters is a rule, whereas for the latter it is an exception regulated by laws which do not permit it to be extended unduly. I will not dwell either on another problem which even so should give pause, namely the reappearance of the *arcana imperii* in the guise of technical experts and technocracy: the technocrat is the repository of knowledge which is not accessible to ordinary people, and which even if made available would not even be understood by most of them, and only a minority (of the subjects of a democratic system) could make any useful contribution to an eventual discussion. In this case it is not a question of the traditional contempt for the common people as an irrational crowd, incapable of making rational decisions even in its own interest, unable to raise its eyes so that instead of staring at the ground of its own daily necessities it might contemplate the blazing sun of the common good. Rather it stems from an objective recognition of its ignorance, or rather its lack of scientific know-how, of the unbridgeable gulf which separates the expert from the lay-man, the competent from the incompetent, the technician's or scientist's laboratory from the high street. I will not dwell on this issue because the conflict between democracy and technocracy belongs to the category of democracy's 'paradoxes' rather than to its failures.

When comparing the ideal model of visible power with the 'actually existing reality' we must bear in mind the tendency, which I have been exploring above, for every form of rule to remove itself from the scrutiny of the ruled either by self-concealment or by concealment, i.e. by using the ploys of secrecy or camouflage.

I will immediately dispense with the second aspect of the problem, because concealment is a phenomenon common to every form of public communication. What used to be called 'simulation' from the point of view of the active subject, the protagonist (i.e. the ruler), is what is now called 'manipulation' seen from the point of view of the passive subjects or victims (i.e. the citizens). I have often had occasion to notice that every problem that concerns the political arena can be considered *ex parte principis* or *ex parte populi*. Political writers for centuries approached political problems from the point of view of the 'prince': hence the interest in the question of the 'useful' lie and in the conditions and limits within which it was legitimate. The same problem considered from the point of view of the receiver of the message becomes the problem of a consensus but extorted by using various forms of manipulation, forms which experts on mass communications have been debating for some time. The most direct heirs of the useful lie in mass societies are ideological systems and their derivatives. Political writers have always known, and nowadays we know better than ever, that political power in the strict sense of the term, whose distinctive instrument is the use of force, cannot do without ideological power, and hence needs 'persuaders', whether overt or hidden. Even the democratic system – and by 'democratic system' here I mean one in which supreme power (supreme in so far as it alone is authorized to use force as a last resort) is exercised in the name of and on behalf of the people by virtue of the procedure of elections based on universal suffrage and held periodically within a fixed time-limit – not only cannot do without ideological power but in certain respects needs it more than the autocrat or the ruling oligarchy, both of whom are dealing with an inert mass deprived of human rights. Democratic writers have always deprecated the 'falsehood' of the ruler with the same fury and the same doggedness as anti-democratic writers have inveighed against the beguiling eloquence of the demagogues. What distinguishes democratic power from autocratic power is that only in the former can unrestricted criticism and licence to express various points of view lead to the development of antibodies within the 'body politic', thus making possible the 'demystification' of the workings of government.[37]

## SUBTERRANEAN GOVERNMENT, CRYPTOGOVERNMENT AND
## ALL-SEEING POWER

The most relevant issue, one which is the acid test for the potential of visible power to eradicate invisible power, concerns the openness of government, the 'publicity' of the proceedings of the political system, which as we have seen, represent the real turning-point in the metamorphosis of the modern state from an absolute state to a constitutional state. Considering the way things are going in Italy, the fact must be faced that the victory over invisible power has not been achieved. Above all I have in mind first the phenomena of '*sottogoverno*', or 'subterranean governments',[38] and secondly what we could term 'cryptogovernment'. This division of power, not according to the classic distinctions between vertical and horizontal power, but in terms of its degree of conspicuousness, i.e. visible (public), semi-submerged (semi-public) and submerged (occult), is not particularly orthodox but may serve to capture aspects of reality which elude the traditional classification.

*Sottogoverno* has so far remained an almost exclusively journalistic phrase, yet it deserves by now to be granted a place within the conceptual apparatus of political scientists. Perhaps the moment has come to attempt a theory of this phenomenon, which so far only exists – and how! – in practice. The practice is intimately bound up with the characteristic function of the post-Keynesian state (and which neo-Marxists call state capitalism), namely the government of the economy. Wherever the state has assumed responsibility for managing the economy, politicians no longer exclusively exercise power through the traditional channels, namely the law, government decrees, and various kinds of administrative measures which have formed part of the sphere of visible power as long as the parliamentary system and the juridical state have been in existence (by the latter I mean a state where proceedings of public administration are subject to legal control). They also wield influence by their control over the major centres of economic power (banks, nationalized industries, state subsidized industries, etc.) which provide the bulk of the funds needed to support the various party machines, while these in turn provide the key to the government's successful election and legitimation.[39] In contrast to traditional legislative and executive power, the management of the economy mainly belongs to the sphere of invisible power in that it is beyond the compass, even if not in theory then in practice, of democratic and jurisdictional control. As far as democratic control is concerned, the problem of the relationship between parliament and the management of the economy

continues to be one of the most serious issues for constitutional theorists, political scientists, and politicians, for the simple reason that
despite some changes, such as the one brought about in Italy by Law
no. 14 of 24 January 1978[39] relating to parliamentary control on
appointments made by public bodies, it is far from being resolved.
Confirmation is provided by the scandals which continue to surface
without warning and confront public opinion with further dis-
concerting revelations pointing not so much to the negligence of
government as to its impotence. As for the jurisdictional control of
administrative proceedings, this elementary observation must
suffice: in the constitutional state administrative justice has been
instituted to safeguard the interests of the citizen with respect to
eventual illegal acts by public administrators, on the assumption that
the citizen is to a greater or lesser extent harmed by such acts. But
when an illegal act by a public official is not prejudicial to the interests
of a citizen but on the contrary promotes them, in other words when
the individual citizen benefits from public illegality, the premiss on
which the institution of administrative justice is based no longer
holds.

I have coined the term 'cryptogovernment' for the totality of
actions carried out by paramilitary political forces which operate
behind the scenes in collaboration with the secret services, or with
sections of them, or at least with their connivance. The first episode
of this type in Italy's recent history was undoubtedly the Piazza
Fontana massacre. Despite the fact that a long judiciary inquiry
ensued, proceeding in several phases and directions, the mystery has
never been cleared up, the truth has not been uncovered, the shrouds
of darkness have never been penetrated. And yet we are not dealing
with the realm of the unknowable. We are dealing with simple fact,
which as such belongs to the sphere of the knowable, so that even if
we do not know *who* it was, we know with certainty that it was
*someone*. I will not hazard any guesses, I will not venture any
hypothesis. I will restrict myself to recalling the suspicion that
lingered at the end of the trial that the principle of official secrets was
used to protect the secrets of the 'anti-state'.[40] I refer back to the
Piazza Fontana massacre at the risk of seeming to be still harping on
an incident which is now remote (though 'removed' rather than
remote), even if it is coming back into the news, because the
degeneration of the Italian political system dates from then, i.e. from
the moment an *arcanum*, in the fullest sense of the term, found its
way, unforeseen and unforeseeable, into Italian social life, and
disrupted it, only to be followed by further episodes just as serious
and which have remained equally obscure. Most human beings have

a poor memory as far as other people's wounds are concerned. There must surely be someone, though, prepared to take on the responsiblity of representing Italy's collective memory and leave no stone unturned which might help Italians to understand. Too many mysterious objects have passed through the country's recent history like ships in the night for the fragility and vulnerability of her democratic institutions not to become apparent to all, even in terms of what I have been trying to elucidate in these pages, namely the opaqueness (opaque in the sense of non-transparent rather than lack-lustre) of power. And then, if the existence of an *arcanum imperii* or *dominationis* remains hypothetical, what is in no way hypothetical but dramatically real is the resurgence, unthinkable till a few years ago, of the *arcana seditionis* often in the form of terrorist attacks. Terrorism is a perfect example of the 'occult' power which runs through the whole of history. One of the fathers of modern terrorism, Bakunin, proclaimed the need for an 'invisible dictatorship'.[41] Whoever decides to join a terrorist group necessarily adopts the subterfuge of a clandestine existence, puts on a disguise, and practises the same art of falsehood described so often as one of the strategems of the Machiavellian prince. The terrorist, too, scrupulously observes the maxim that the more that power is able to know, see, recognize without being seen, the more effective it is.

Before I close, may I be permitted an allusion to another leitmotif which runs parallel to that of invisible power, namely the question of the 'all-seeing power'. Bentham himself, as we have seen, had fully realized the limits of his building scheme when he wrote that its principle was indeed applicable to institutions other than the prison, but only 'within the confines of a fairly limited space'. Curiously the upper limit of the Panopticon's effectiveness was the same as the one Rousseau envisaged for direct democracy. But now it is no longer in the realm of science fiction to imagine direct democracy being made possible by means of computer technology. And if so why should not the same type of computer technology make it possible to provide those in power with a similar detailed of our private lives, even in a mass society? The knowledge that absolute monarchs such as Louis XIII or Louis XIV had about their subjects bears no comparison with what a well-organized state can obtain about its own citizens. When we read the accounts of *jacqueries* in the past we realize just how little the monarch was able to 'see' with his apparatus of state servants, and how revolts broke out without the ruler, no matter how absolute, being able to prevent them (even if he was not very subtle in the way he went about putting them down). What a small amount of power when compared to the enormous possibilities opening up for a state which has at its disposal huge electronic brains. Whether this scenario is destined to become reality or remain a nightmare, no one as yet can say. In any event it should be seen as a trend completely at variance with the one which inspired the ideal of democracy as the apotheosis of visible power: it is a trend not towards the maximum control of power on the part of citizens, but on the contrary towards the maximum control of the subjects on the part of those in power.

# 5

# Liberalism Old and New

The last few years in Italy, and not just in Italy, have seen a rekindling of interest in liberal thought and its history. The *Centro Einaudi* in Turin has played a prominent role in fostering this interest with publications which make a serious contribution to the scholarship on the subject. One of the most notable examples is the quarterly *The Library of Liberty*, number 76 of which (Jan.–Mar. 1980) was dedicated to the memory of its founder, Fulvio Guerrini and entitled 'La libertà dei contemporanei' (i.e. 'Contemporary Liberty', which ought to be distinct from the liberty of classical times, the modern age and of our descendents). It contained articles by Dahrendorf and Sartori, by Matteucci and Pasquino, by Georgio Galli and Urbani, by Ricossa and Giovane Zincone, and can be seen as a synoptic view of the trends and prospects of neo-liberalism. The *Centre* is also responsible for the volumes published in the series '*Quaderni*' which has introduced to an Italian reading public such authors as Milton Friedman, Samuel Brittan, James Buchanan, William Niskanen, who for some time now have been at the centre of lively debate especially in the United States. The periodical *Libro aperto* or *Open Book* has been appearing twice-yearly since 1980, giving news on various liberal and neo-liberal movements in the world. In 1981 alone a spate of books were published on the subject within a few months of each other including Ettore Cuomo's *Profile of European Liberalism* Giuseppe Pezzino's, *Ethics and Politics in the Liberal Crisis*, Nadia Boccara's *Victorians and Radicals. From Mill to Russell*. There was also *Liberalism in a Threatened Democracy* by Nicola Matteucci, a scholar who throughout all the years he has devoted to the defence of the liberal tradition, (largely in the form of eulogies to his favourite author, Tocqueville), has always been in the firing line to combat 'the three extreme evils': communism, socialism and populist democracy. While I was writing these pages in 1981

Laterza brought out a new book by Dahrendorf, intriguingly called, *The New Liberty: Survival and Justice in a Changing World* (with an introduction in the Italian edition by Lucio Coletti), and Armando published a compilation of various articles under the catchy title *Free Freedom*, which opens with the *Manifesto of Liberty* by Jean-Claude Colli.[1]

<h2>A LEFT-WING VIEW OF JOHN STUART MILL</h2>

But the real surprise was the reprinting of a liberal classic such as *On Liberty* by John Stuart Mill, in a new series, '*Lo spazio politico*', edited by Giulio Giorello and Marco Mondadori.[2] 'The Political Space' has a left-wing orientation, though this is an undogmatic Left which is prepared to come to terms with the enlightened Right (Luhmann) and take on board writers who were once beyond the pale (Carl Schmitt). The two editors, both celebrated philosophers of science and pupils of the founding father of modern scientific methodology, Ludovico Geymonat (who would probably have excommunicated them politically), discovered Mill's political liberalism via the methodological libertarianism of Feyerabend (and hence found themselves confronting such issues as the relationship between the philosophy of science and political philosophy, one which deserves thorough investigation). Once they were convinced via their reading of Mill and Feyerabend of the fertility of conflict and dissent, of a plurality of points of view, they came to the conclusion that the Left was in need of a genuine 'Copernican revolution'. This would consist in transcending the dogma of centralization and the recognition of the social system as a totality of interactions between groups with utility functions (the phrase is taken from J. C. Harsanyi) which, as such, precludes any concentration of power claiming to organize social life according to a uniform plan (and here I am quoting none other than the doyen of *laissez-faire* market economists, Friedrich von Hayek).

A new edition of Mill, coming as it did out of the blue, could not fail to provoke a host of reactions and comments, some of them delighted, others irritated, others perplexed or actually highly polemical.[3] As for myself, this unexpected and startling espousal of Mill by writers who persist in considering themselves on the Left made me aware of a curious role reversal which has taken place between two generations who have lived through different historical situations. I remember the zeal and excitement felt by those of us who during the last years of Fascism had never left the fold of the liberal tradition (kept alive with dignity and effectiveness by the likes of Croce,[4] Einaudi, Salvatorelli[5] and Omodeo[6]) when we rediscovered Marx: the extraordinary forcefulness in the way he called into question received truths, his ability to make us see history from the vantage point of those who had never had 'their' history, his ferocious critique of ideologies as masks donned to conceal the lust for power and wealth. Is it any wonder if today, after such a surfeit of hyper-theoretical and tediously repetitive Marxist dogma, and now that the revolutions carried out in the name of Marx have produced despotic regimes, a new generation animated by a critical spirit and iconoclastic mentality (1968 was not in vain!) is rediscovering liberal writers? As may be known already, the most famous Italian edition of Mill's essay on liberty was the one produced by Piero Gobetti at the time Fascism was imposing an illiberal state on the country (1924).[7] Gobetti persuaded one of his masters to write the preface – Luigi Einaudi, the most erudite and unfaltering voice of Italian *laissez-faire* liberalism. Gobetti, however, was to write in the same year a brief but trenchant article entitled '*L'ora di Marx*' ('Marx's Hour') which finished with these prophetic words: 'It is unlikely that the Fascist parenthesis will be of short duration: but it will certainly be in the name of Marx that the proletarian avant-garde and their intransigent elites will bury it together with its illusions.'[8] As we can see, politics moves, like the Lord, in a mysterious way. The history of ideas proceeds via a continual reshuffling of cards which allows us to indulge in any number of games without being able to foresee the outcome of any of them.

Of course, I can only welcome with open arms the fact that two left-wing intellectuals have closely re-read one of the classic texts of liberalism and recommend it as a prescribed text to their fellow travellers. It may herald the end of the mutual mistrust that has existed between the liberal and socialist political cultures. Marxists have often had good reason to deplore the superficiality and bias to be detected in Marx's detractors. But liberals have been forced to protest equally justifiably against the summary liquidition of the great achievements of liberal thought, often contemptuously dismissed as a by-product of bourgeois interests (naturally considered 'tainted'). For someone who has continued to read the liberal classics, even in unpropitious times, without ever considering them a dead letter (and a dead letter they have been for the whole Italian Marxist-Leninist tradition which embraced Rousseau but not Locke, Hegel but not Kant), the revival of Mill by the Left is something that can only be welcomed. The ideas so happily expressed by Mill – concerning the need for there to be limits to power, even when this power is the power of the majority, concerning the fruitfulness of conflict, the praise of diversity, the condemnation of conformism, the absolute priority accorded by a well-governed society to the freedom of opinion – became common places in the nineteenth-century political journalism of civilized countries. Re-reading the introduction by Giorello and Mondadori to their book, I was prompted to muse on what a dense shroud of darkness must have enveloped these ideas in the intellectual tradition of the European Left, if, when brought to light once more, they can be presented as a revelation. I thought of Carlo Cattaneo who devoted all his life and many talents to investigating and popularizing his doctrine of antithesis as the mainspring of progress and of the state as an 'immense transaction'.[9] From Popper's theory of the open society onwards, the opposition closed/open has supplanted the dichotomy of light and dark pioneered by the Enlightenment. By the mid-nineteenth century Cattaneo was already arguing that where a society is founded on a single, exclusive doctrine it will be closed and hence static, and where there is a plurality of doctrines in permanent and fruitful rivalry with each other, the system will be open and progressive. He wrote that stationary civilizations, such as the 'Chinese', are closed systems. Dynamic civilizations, like Ancient Rome and the Britain of his day, are open systems. And in answer to the question he posed himself concerning how closed systems may become open, he replied that it could come about through the 'grafting on' of alien doctrines which upset the original equilibrium. Mill also inherited the traditional image of China as a 'static' society and formed the opinion that if it was to progress 'it will have to be with the help of foreigners.'[10] As for the subject of conflict, Cattaneo had the following to say: 'From the perpetual friction between ideas the European genius is still being kept aflame today'.[11]

### LIBERAL STATE AND SOCIAL STATE

Certainly Mill's essay is the 'ABC' of liberalism. But after 'ABC' come, as the ensuing fifty years was to show, all the other letters of the alphabet. What is more we have not yet got to 'Z'. My ideas here converge with those of Frederico Stame, who has written that the task of reconstructing a new doctrine of liberty is more arduous than a nineteenth-century utilitarian thinker (and one with a Eurocentric bias) could have possibly imagined,[12] and, I might add, more arduous than is realized by those strenuous advocates of monetarism who have decreed the death of the Welfare State.

The principle of justice which is Mill's sticking-point is that of *neminem laedere*, i.e. do harm to no one: 'The only purpose for which power may legitimately be exercised over any member of a civilized society against his will is to avoid causing harm to others.'[13] But as we all know, after the *neminem laedere* (do harm to no one) comes *suum cuique tribuere*, or render to each his own. In his commentary on the *praecepta iuris* of Roman jurists, Leibniz (what old stuff!) remarked that the first precept was sufficient to regulate the *ius proprietatis* but that regulation of the *ius societatis* needed the second as well. How can society hold together, in reality, without a criterion of fair distribution? Besides, Mill himself recognizes in a passage where, taking up these issues at the end of the essay, he maintains that the conduct which government can impose consists first ('first', mind) 'in not injuring the interests of one another', but goes on to say that, second, government must ensure 'each person's bearing his share (to be fixed *on some equitable principle*) of the labours and sacrifices incurred for defending the society or its members from injury and molestation [my emphasis]'[14] I have emphasized the phrase 'on the basis of the principle of equality.' But what are these 'equitable' principles, if not principles of fair distribution?

Despite the idea, recurrent in modern philosophy of law (up to and including Hegel), that law, in contrast to morality, consists of negative precepts, the principal of which is *neminem laedere*, every juridical system, even the one which would be the basis of an ideal liberal state (which has never existed in reality), consists of negative and positive precepts. The idea that the sole task of the state is to prevent individuals causing harm to each other, an idea which is taken to its logical and austere extremes in the uncompromising liberalism of Herbert Spencer, stems from an arbitrary reduction of all public law to penal law (which gives rise to the image of the night-watchman state). As I have had occasion to say in the most diverse contexts, the transition from the *laissez-faire* liberal state to the social-liberal state is epitomized by the shift from a negative to a positive legal apparatus, from one with a predominantly protective-repressive function to one designed to foster or promote the features of an ideal society.[15] But this is not to make out that there has ever been a state which limited itself to simple prevention without also extending its sphere of action to promoting behaviour conducive to harmonious coexistence or to sheer survival, e.g. by encouraging civil defence initiatives as advocated by Mill. At least, this is true from the moment the state has not only to protect individuals from each other but all individuals collectively from the potential aggression of another state. Whatever the case may be: whether the positive function of the state is large or small (not only prevention but promotion, not only affording protection but also creating incentives), the principle of 'commutative justice' (to take up a traditional category which has lost none of its relevance) which consists of making a good (or bad) deed correspond to an equal and fitting reward (or punishment) in accordance with the principle of arithmetic equivalence, will no longer suffice. For any society to hold together, it is essential that some elements of distributive justice are also introduced. And as everyone knows, this is where the problems start. Distribute, yes, but using what criteria? The current debate on the Welfare State arises from the divergent answers to this simple question.

Not that it is even easy to determine the correspondence between personal injury and compensation, between crime and punishment. The profound changes that have occured in the history of how punishment is conceived and should be meted out illustrate this clearly enough. It is no simple matter either deciding in the first place what constitutes personal injury (just think of the health risks caused by industrial pollution) or crime (consider the problem posed by so called civil disobedience, where it is so difficult to draw the line between legal and illegal behaviour). But I have no need to labour the point that when it is a question of distributing burdens or rewards things get horribly complicated. Here, just as in the case of commutative justice, the problems are twofold: what is to be distributed and using what criteria? But at least in the situation where commutative justice presides over transactions, the first question, namely what should be done by the state, calls forth the traditional answer endorsed by Mill, 'It should repress harmful conduct', which even if only at a high level of generality has the merit of being unambiguous and universally acceptable – except to those who believe that the state should also repress immoral conduct irrespective of harm done to others. (I recall that Mill's essay made a timely contribution a few years ago to a widely publicized dispute between English jurists and philosophers when it was quoted in order to repudiate the thesis ascribing to criminal law a normative moral function).[16] In contrast, when appeal is made to distributive justice it is neither obvious nor universally agreed what is to be distributed and according to what criteria. Simplifying the issue, though not drastically, it could be said that this is the dividing line between advocates of the (classical liberal) *laissez-faire* state and advocates of the (social-liberal) Welfare State. In the sphere of civil and criminal law of advanced nations, i.e. in the parts of the system where commutative (or corrective) justice is applied, there are common patterns which can profitably be compared. But in the same countries, when it comes to the distribution of burdens and rewards, the most contrasting ideas collide and conflict, locked in a feud which apparently offers no way out.

## WHICH LIBERALISM?

When we speak of a renewed interest in liberal thought we must be careful to make sure we are talking about the same thing. The question I raised a few years ago about socialism can be asked just as well about liberalism. Which liberalism? It can be investigated in the same way as any ideology generally is, by providing answers on such points as when it originated, what its main variants or 'schools' have been, which authors play a major role in its evolution etc. However, in contrast to socialism, which for the last century or so has been identified with the work of one thinker (so much so that the comparison is not so much between liberalism and socialism as between liberalism and Marxism), liberalism is a movement in the history of ideas which develops via a host of writers quite distinct from each other, such as Locke, Montesquieu, Kant, Adam Smith, Humboldt, Constant, John Stuart Mill, Tocqueville, just to cite some of the tradition's pantheon of classical thinkers. But no matter how many facets of liberal doctrine can be brought to light by consulting different authors in turn, I believe that for my present purposes, since it is a sound principle not to multiply entities unnecessarily, its defining features and the ones which should always be uppermost in mind concern what it has to say in two areas: economics and politics. As an economic theory liberalism is the upholder of the market economy; as a political theory, it upholds the principle of the state which governs as little as possible, or as it is now expressed, of the minimal state (i.e. reduced to the minimum necessary).

The connections between the two theories are obvious. Certainly one of the ways to reduce the state to a bare minimum is to take away from it control over economic and business activity, which would mean making the intervention of politics in economic affairs the exception rather than the rule. However the two theories are independent from each other and we would do well to consider them separately. They are independent because the theory concerning the limits of state power does not only refer to intervention in economics but also extends to the spiritual sphere, that of ethics and religion. From this point of view the liberal state is also a lay state, i.e. a state which does not identify itself with a specific religious denomination (nor with a specific philosophical world-view as the foundation of political theory, as does Marxism-Leninism), even if a state can be secular, and hence agnostic in religious and philosophical matters and still be interventionist in economics. While it is difficult to imagine a liberal state which is not at the same time the champion of economic free enterprise, and inconceivable that a state could be liberal without being secular, it is perfectly conceivable for a secular state to be neither liberal nor based on *laissez-faire*, as is the case of a social democratic government.

With the liberal conception of the state what finally comes to be recognized both intellectually and constitutionally, and thus laid down in basic rules, is the distinction and line of demarcation between the state and the 'non-state', and by non-state I mean religious society, the general intellectual and moral life of individuals and groups, and civil society (or the realm of productive relations in Marxist terms). The dual process of the formation of the liberal state can be described on the one hand as the emancipation of political from religious power (the secular state), and on the other as the emancipation of economic power from political power (the *laissez-faire* state). Via the first process of emancipation the state ceases to be the secular arm of the church, while via the second it becomes the secular arm of commercial and entrepreneurial bourgeoisie. The liberal state is one which has consented to the loss of its monopoly of ideological power by conceding civil rights, foremost among which was the right to freedom in religion and political opinion, and to the loss of its economic power by conceding economic freedom, and has ended up retaining solely the monopoly of legitimate force, whose exercise is however limited by its recognition of the rights of man and by the various legal constraints which historically gave rise to the *Rechtsstaat* or juridical state. By means of the monopoly of legitimate force, legitimate because regulated by laws (this is the rational-legal state described by Max Weber), the state has to ensure the free circulation of ideas, and hence safeguard society from domination by any sectarian religion or orthodoxy, and guarantee the free circulation of wealth and hence put an end to the interference of the state in the economy. Characteristic of the liberal doctrine in politics and economics is a negative conception of the state, reduced to being no more than an instrument for the realization of individual ends, and by contrast a positive conception of the non-state, conceived as the sphere in which individuals, through dealings with their fellow human beings, mould, develop and perfect their own personality.

I am well aware that apart from economic and political liberalism it is customary to talk of an ethical liberalism, but this is only a precondition of the other two, and one which in this context can be best considered an unspoken assumption. By ethical liberalism is meant the doctrine which accords pride of place in the scale of moral values to the individual, and hence individual freedom in the dual sense of negative and positive freedom. The demand for economic freedom as well as the demand for political freedom are practical consequences, translatable into legal and institutional terms, of the axiomatic primacy of the individual. When we speak of liberalism, and this is just as true of socialism, we are referring to a complex of ideas which concern the organization and regulation of practical existence, and in particular of the social dimension of life. Since one person's assertion of freedom always results in the restriction of someone else's freedom, and since mankind is destined to live in a world of consumer goods and limited resources, the ethical postulate of individual freedom may be valid as an inspiring ideal but must be applied to concrete cases if it is not to remain an abstraction. In this sense the problem which liberalism is called upon to resolve as an economic and political doctrine is how to make it possible for various freedoms to coexist without encroaching on each other, which translates into the formulation and application of practical rules of conduct, in other words in the advocation of a certain kind of economic system and a certain kind of political system.

## THE CRITIQUE OF ACTUALLY EXISTING SOCIALISM

This insistence on the dual aspect of liberalism is justified by the nature of the problem I have undertaken to explore. In fact the revival of interest in liberal thought has two sides: on the one hand it is the assertion of the advantages of the free-market economy over the interventionist state, and on the other it is the assertion of human rights to combat any new form of despotism.

They are two sides which are complementary but can also exist independently, because they relate to two different areas of social reality. But what concerns me here is to point out that both these sets of claims are now being polemically directed against the only two forms of socialism which have so far been realized: the first against social democracy, the second against the socialism of countries dominated by the Soviet Union. Seen in historical terms, therefore, the rediscovery of liberalism could be interpreted as a come-back being staged by *real* liberalism, once given up as dead, against *real* socialism, in its only two historical permutations, namely the social democracy which gave rise to the Welfare State, and communism, which produced a new type of illiberal state in the Soviet Union and in its imitations which have been more or less foisted on other nations. In the last century the diatribes of socialists against liberals were based on the contrast between a project for an ideal society and an existing social reality, and it was a contrast which worked in favour of someone who showed up the evils of the present by outlining the presumed benefits promised by a future society which existed only in the imagination. But after the First World War, and even more so after the Second World War, socialism became a reality, or went a long way towards becoming one, and can now be contested on the same terms as it contested the liberal state in the nineteenth century, namely by appealing not to theory but practice (and malpractice).

Until a few years ago it was above all political liberalism which maintained a polemical onslaught against the wanton destruction of human rights perpetrated by Stalinism and fought to refute the thesis that human rights, being the fruit of the Third Estate's struggles against absolute monarchies, are conceived purely for the defence of bourgeois self-interest and therefore not universally valid (since then even the theory that these rights have a purely bourgeois origin has been refuted). It cannot be denied that this battle did achieve some results, notably in the emergence of the 'revised' (in the non-Marxist sense of the term!) form of communism known as Euro-communism. Over the last few years, however, it is economic liberalism which has made its presence felt. Its target is less the collectivism of countries where communist parties have taken over, than the Welfare State, i.e. the social democratic experiment. In a way the attack on the Soviet system has become taken for granted. What now rouses the fighting passions of the new liberals are the effects, considered by them disastrous, of Keynesian politics, adopted by economically and politically advanced nations particularly at the instigation of social democratic or labour parties. The vices which were traditionally attributed to absolute states – bureaucratization, loss of personal liberties, the waste of resources, poor economic performance – are now attributed point by point to governments which have adopted social democratic or labour-style policies. According to the neo-liberals, whoever thinks it is possible to distinguish good from bad socialism should think again. Everything that even remotely smacks of socialism, even in its most watered-down form (and which socialists do not consider socialist) stinks, and should be thrown out. Accordingly those who were reckless enough to think that the rights concerning economic freedom had to be dropped from the category of basic human rights (as in fact they were from the 'Universal Declaration of the Rights of Man', which had to find a compromise between conflicting demands), ought now to realize the error of their ways. They ought to be convinced, as neo-liberals see it, given the record of those governments which have faithfully applied interventionist policies with the object of creating a Welfare State, that without economic freedom there is no freedom, and the road which opens up is, in the phrase which formed the title of the book by von Hayek, 'the road to serfdom'. (Besides, the indissoluble link between political liberalism and *laissez-faire* economics was central to the position defended by Einaudi in his famous controversy with Croce in the late 1920s.)[17]

In the face of such a major offensive, it is the social democrats who are suffering the greater set-back. At first, following the failure of wholesale collectivism in the Eastern bloc, they had believed they could defend themselves with sound emprirical arguments against attacks from the Left, and that they were thus in a position to fight off accusations that they had stopped short of pursuing the ultimate goal of a socialist society and accepted a *modus vivendi* with capitalism. Now, however, the most insidious threat is coming from the Right, which considers that even the Welfare State is doomed to failure – that is, if it has not failed already – and that social democracy is moving along the road which leads to totalitarianism, despite its own claims not to have succumbed to the temptations dictatorship offered as a short cut to achieving its goals (something that can not be said of its fraternal enemy, communism). In this way the social democrat is caught in a cross-fire. It often happens that someone who tries to appease two conflicting parties ends up feeding the discontent of both. Over the years we have read countless pages, increasingly well documented and increasingly polemical, on the contemporary crisis of the state, which is presented as a capitalist state thinly disguised as a Welfare State, and on the hypocritical integration of the working class which has delivered it into the clutches of the multinationals. Now we are reading other pages of a different kind, no less erudite and well informed, on the contemporary crisis of the state, which is now portrayed as a socialist state thinly disguised as a liberal one, and that under the pretext of social justice (Hayek claims not to know really what this might be)[18] is destroying personal freedom and reducing the individual to a child guided from table to tomb by a chaperone holding his hand, not just mothering him but smothering him. This is a situation which is as paradoxical as it is grotesque. How else is a situation to be described in which the same form of state, and it is important to bear in mind that this is the form of state which has been establishing itself almost universally in democratic countries, finds itself being condemned as capitalist by Marxists old and new, and as socialist by Liberals old and new? There are two possible explanations: either these terms –

capitalism, socialism etc. – have been worn so thin with use that they cannot be used any longer without creating confusion, or else the dual criticism is only apparently contradictory, because in actual fact the Welfare State has been (and will continue to be for many years, I suppose) a compromise solution, one which, like all compromise solutions, lends itself to being repudiated by both conflicting parties.

If two people make out a shape in the distance and one says it is a man and the other that it is a horse, before jumping to the conclusion that neither of them are capable of telling the difference between a man and a horse, it is legitimate to postulate that what they have seen is a centaur (then again, it could be argued that since centaurs do not exist, both of them were mistaken).

### CORSI AND *RICORSI*

The partial success of the *laissez-faire* liberal offensive against the welfare state raises a curious problem relating to the philosophy of history, especially for the Left. The working-class movement originated in the last century under the aegis of a progressive and deterministic conception of history. Progressive in the sense that the course of history was thought to be unfolding in such a way that every new phase compared to its predecessor represented another step forward on the path that led from barbarism to civilization. Deterministic in that every phase is pre-ordained as part of a rational (or providential) scheme and is thus bound to come about. Within this conception of history, socialism has always been held to constitute a new phase of historical development about whose inevitability and intrinsic progressiveness the political parties representing the working-class movement has never had any doubts.

Instead what has happened? Wherever socialism has been achieved it turns out to be very difficult to interpret it as a progressive phase of history: at most it might be considered such in the case of those developing countries where it has succeeded in establishing itself. Where it has not been achieved, or achieved only half-way, as in the Welfare State, not only is it difficult to see how the other half can be made up in the short term, but everything points to the fact that a strong trend is gathering momentum towards abandoning that half of the territory already gained. It has been argued that the expectations frustrated by the bourgeois revolution, which claimed to be universal (i.e. not the emancipation of a class but of mankind) but turned out not to be, were channelled into the critiques of society formulated by the various socialist schools of thought, first and foremost Marxism. If this is true, it is equally true that the expectations disappointed by the outcome of socialism, whether total or partial, have induced not the belief in another instalment in the progress of history, one which no one so far has been able to foresee or even outline for us, but the temptation to turn back. When those who have ventured into a labyrinth (the image of the labyrinth is coming into fashion) notice they have finished up in a dead end, they retrace their steps. Retracing their steps it may happen that they realize they were going the right way and they were wrong to give up. It is in this sense that the words of the neo-liberal economists are to be understood: for them, when it comes to the crunch, capitalism is the lesser evil because it is the system in which power is most widely dispersed and each individual has the greatest number of alternatives.

In this way a progressive and determinist conception of history is replaced by a cyclical and indeterminist one (based on trial and error) in which once the cycle is complete it starts all over again. This idea of a return to the beginning fits into the historical category of a 'restoration' myth. Moreover it was precisely in the 'Restoration' period that liberalism experienced its golden age of intellectual vitality (what Croce called the age of the 'religion of liberty').[19] Naturally to talk nowadays of a restoration is premature. Faced with restoration governments like those of Thatcher or Reagan, all we can say is 'wait and see': *respice finem*. Apart from anything else, the concept of restoration presupposes a highly simplistic, dualistic theory of history, consisting of monotonous alternations of positive and negative phases. In the light of a more complex conception of history, one which also reflects more accurately the reality of how history develops, there is a tendency to interpret neo-liberalism as a third stage, a sort of negation of the negation in the dialectical sense, in which nothing of what was positive in the second stage is lost. This is how the assertions of the new generation of economists are to be understood to the effect that they do not deny the existence of the needs which were the starting point for the Welfare State, the need for greater equality, for poverty to be combatted etc., what they reject is the means used to meet them, proposing in their place alternative strategies, such as negative income tax or the distribution of coupons for social services.

*Respice finem*. Under both headings, economic and political, liberalism is the doctrine of the minimal state: the state is a necessary evil but an evil nonetheless. We cannot do without the state, and thus anarchy is not contemplated, but the area of society which falls within the compass of political power (which is the power to put people in jail) is to be reduced to an absolute minimum. Contrary to what is usually alleged, the antithesis of the liberal state is not the absolute state, if by absolute state is meant the state in which the power of the sovereign is not controlled by representative assemblies, (i.e where power is transmitted from the top to the bottom of a hierarchy). The antithesis of an absolute state is the democratic state, or more precisely the representative state which, via the progressive extension of political rights to the point where universal suffrage is achieved, gradually transforms itself into a democratic state. The antithesis of the liberal state is the paternalistic state which takes care of its subjects as if they were eternally under age, and provides for their happiness. This rejection of paternalism is made abundantly clear by the first classical thinkers of liberalism: Locke, Kant, Humboldt and, naturally, Adam Smith, so much so that none of these early champions of liberalism can be included in the ranks of democratic writers. This is equally true the other way round: Rousseau cannot be counted as a liberal theorist. The state which these first liberals fought tooth and nail was the so-called *Wohlfahrtsstaat*, in other words the Welfare State of the day, German version. Certainly the 'welfare' the leading reformers at the time were advocating amounted to very little compared to what democratic systems provide in the modern age. But among the first liberal writers the terms of the debate were not very different from those used by contemporary liberals, who persist in the belief that the best welfare is what individuals are able to secure for themselves as long as they are free to pursue their own interests. As I have earlier invoked the philosophy of history, what naturally comes to mind is Vico's concept of *corsi* and *ricorsi*,the cyclic ebbs and flows of cultural life.[20] The minimal state was originally part of a rebellion against the paternalistic state of enlightened princes. The minimal state is now being proposed once again to combat the Welfare State, which is accused of reducing the free citizen to the status of a protected subject: in a word to combat new forms of paternalism.

THE POLITICAL MARKET

But the paternalistic state of today is the creation not of an enlightened despot but of democratic governments. The whole difference lies here and it is a crucial one. It is a crucial difference because Enlightenment liberal doctrine had a field-day fighting paternalism along with absolutism, and thus simultaneously advancing two causes: emancipation of civil society from political power (the market from the state as we would say nowadays) and the establishment of the representative state (upholding parliament against the monarchy). But today this two-pronged attack would inevitably lead to the end of democracy (and the first symptoms of this are already with us).

That the aberrant development of the Welfare State, as is it now widely considered to be, is closely bound up with the development of democracy is beyond doubt. It has been said, and repeated so often that it is now actually a cliché, that the 'overloading' caused by the excessive demands made of government in advanced societies, from which derives one of the reasons for their becoming 'ungovernable', is a characteristic of democratic regimes where people can come together, associate, and organize so as to make their voice heard, and where they have the right, if not actually to take the decisions themselves on matters which concern them, then at least to choose periodically the persons they consider best in a position to look after their own interests.[21] The 'service state', which as such grows ever more bureaucratized, came about as a response, now criticized with the wisdom of hindsight, to the justified demands being made from below. Nowadays people make out that the fruits of this initiative were poisonous, but that we should recognize that the tree was only capable of producing this type of fruit. Personally I do not believe this (thus I do not agree with those who would like to pull the tree out by its roots). Perhaps the presence of social democratic parties in certain countries may have accelerated the hypertrophy of the state, but the phenomenon is a general one. The country where the Welfare State is today the target of more ferocious criticism than anywhere else is the United States, which has never had a social democratic party. In Italy the Welfare State grew up in the shade of Christian Democrat administrations, of governments headed by the middle classes. When the only ones to be granted political rights were property owners, it was natural for the main demand made of the state to be for the protection of property rights and rights of contract. Once political rights were extended to include the destitute and the illiterate it became equally natural that those in power, who besides made themselves out to be (and in a certain sense were) the representatives of the people, should be asked for work, provisions for those who cannot work, free schooling and, in the course of time (and why not?), cheap housing, medical services etc. Our Constitution is not a socialist constitution, but all these demands have come to be recognized as the most natural things in the world, and have actually been translated into rights.

If this nexus between the process of democratization and the growth of the Welfare State is looked at not only from the point of view of the ruled, i.e. those who make demands of the state, but also from that of the rulers, i.e. those who have to respond to them, the same conclusion is reached. It is above all to economists that we owe the discovery and elaboration of the analogy between democracy and the market-place. It is an analogy which must be treated with the utmost caution given the number of specious parallels and substantial differences it involves. But there is a lot to be said for Max Weber's idea, taken up, developed and popularized by Schumpeter, that the political leader is comparable to an entrepreneur, whose profit is power, whose power is measured in votes, whose votes depend on an ability to satisfy the demands of the electors and whose ability to do this depends on the public resources at his disposal.[22] The interest of the citizen to obtain favours from the state is matched by the interest of the politician, whether elected or standing for election, to grant them. Between the two there is formed a perfect relationship of *do ut des*: the one confers power by exercising the vote, the other distributes advantages or eliminates anomalies by exercising the power he has been given. It goes without saying that not everyone's wishes can be met, but as in the economic arena, so too in the political arena some are stronger than others, and the shrewdness of the politician consists, just as in business, in being able to gauge the tastes of the public, and if posible even to manipulate them. In the political arena too there are winners and losers, those for whom business is going well and lame ducks, but the fact that the political arena is managed according to the ground rules of constitutional democracy which give everyone a say and allow everyone to organize and make their presence felt, makes it all the more necessary for the organizers of the spectacle to improve the quality of the performances so as to win applause for their efforts.

If the core principle of liberal doctrine is the theory of the minimal state, the practical implementation of democracy, which is after all a historical consequence of liberalism or at least a historical extension of it (even if not all states which were originally liberal have turned into democratic ones, all the democratic states which are now in existence were originally liberal), has led to a form of state which is no longer minimal even if it is not the maximal state of totalitarian regimes. The political market-place, if we want to persist in using this analogy, has superimposed itself on the economic market-place, thus correcting or corrupting it according to which way you look at it. The basic question is thus whether it is possible to return to the economic market-place, as the neo-liberals insist, without reforming the political market-place, or even abolishing it altogether. If it cannot be abolished, at least its sphere of activity is to be reduced. The political proposals of these neo-liberals all point in this direction, and adopt as their logical framework the classic doctrine of the natural limits of state power, which applies in their eyes irrespective of whether the power of the state is, as in democratic systems, the power of the people rather than of an autocrat.

## ARE LIBERALISM AND DEMOCRACY COMPATIBLE?

I do not intend to go into the merits of neo-liberal policies, because this issue has been debated extensively over the last few years.[23] What I am concerned to do here is to highlight the fact that though democracy has, for the last century at least, been considered the natural progression from liberalism, the two ideologies prove to be no longer compatible at all once democracy has been taken to its logical extremes as a mass democracy, or rather as a democracy of mass parties, so as to produce the Welfare State. If the banks which were theoretically supposed to confine the state have burst, it is difficult to deny that what happened is that they were swept away by the flood of popular political participation which was unleashed by universal suffrage. It has often been said that the Keynesian economic strategy was an attempt to save capitalism without abandoning democracy, so rejecting the two opposite solutions of either destroying capitalism by sacrificing democracy ( Leninism in practice) or destroying democracy so as to save capitalism (fascism). It might now be said that for the liberals of the new generation the problem is the other way round, that of saving (if it is still possible and as far as it is possible), democracy without abandoning capitalism. Whereas during the Great Depression of the 1930s it had looked as if it was capitalism which was precipitating a crisis in democracy, it seems to them now that democracy is precipitating a crisis in capitalism.

I prefer to formulate the problem in these terms rather than in those of the relationship between 'state and market'. I prefer not to use this phrase because the term 'state' is too abstract. There are various forms of state. In the stereotyped language current in certain left-wing circles in Italy it has become in vogue to talk about the 'state matrix' (what is more 'party matrix') as if all forms of state were the same (and all parties the same). Expressions like 'state matrix' and 'party matrix' only serve to obscure (I would not go so far as to say wilfully) the fact that political power can be exercised in various ways, and it is necessary actually to decide on which one is to be preferred to the others in order not to end up with a wishy-washy, half-baked anarchism (which is equally true for the choice of which party programme to support). It is all very well saying that the state, like the market economy, is a form of social control. But the social control peculiar to a democratic state is not the same as that of an autocratic state. This accounts for the fact that what is at issue these days is not the general relationship between the state and the market-place, but the specific relationship between the market-place and the democratic state, or then again between the economic market and the political market. The crisis in the Welfare State is also the result of the contrast, which neither liberals, marxists nor genuine democrats had previously taken sufficiently into account, between the economic entrepreneur concerned with the maximization of profit and the political entrepreneur concerned with the maximization of power through the winning of support. That a conflict may arise between the interests that these two parties are pursuing is something which is now being brought out clearly in the argument over the ungovernability of democracies, i.e. of those societies where the arena in which political contest takes place can be likened to the market-place. What is more, there is no invisible hand hovering above the two of them to harmonize their interests, despite their wishes. What the demands of neo-liberalism boil down to is for the tension between the two to be reduced by cutting the politician's nails while leaving all the business executive's talons razor sharp. In short, for neo-liberals democracy is ungovernable not only with respect to the voting public, due to the excess of unsatisfiable demands they make, but also with respect to those in power, because they are forced to meet the bulk of them so that their enterprise (the party) will prosper.

One way of understanding the present liberal revival is by seeing it in terms of its historical progression (or regression), which can be summed up as follows: in the past the liberal crusade was directed against socialism, which in its collectivist version (which is anyway the most authentic one) is its natural enemy. In the last few years it has also been directed against the Welfare State, i.e. against the watered-down version of socialism (which according to one section of the Left is also a travesty of it). Now what is coming under attack is democracy pure and simple. There is a great danger here. Not only is the Welfare State jeopardized, in other words the great historical compromise between the working-class movement and advanced capitalism, but democracy itself is at stake, i.e. the other great historical compromise which preceded it between the traditional privileges of the propertied classes and the world of organized labour, which gave birth directly or indirectly to modern democracy (via universal suffrage, the formation of mass parties etc.).

The complex set of issues involved can also be presented in different terms: the antithesis minimal state/maximal state, which is the aspect of the controversy most frequently discussed, is not to be confused with the antithesis strong state/weak state. Two different oppositions are involved which do not necessarily overlap. The charge which neo-liberalism makes against the Welfare State is not just that it has violated the principle of the minimal state but also that it has given rise to a state which is no longer capable of carrying out its proper function, which is to govern (the weak state). The ideal of neo-liberalism thus becomes one of a state which is both minimal and strong. Incidentally, the fact that the two antitheses are not to be equated is illustrated by the spectacle Italians constantly have going on in front of their eyes of a state which is simultaneously maximal and weak.

## A NEW SOCIAL CONTRACT

I said that the danger is great. For me the danger is great not only for party political reasons, but also for philosophical reasons in the widest sense. I will explain. Liberal thought continues to thrive, even assuming new forms which may disconcert by their regressive, and in many respects overtly reactionary character (one cannot fail to detect the vindictiveness which creeps into the current campaign to dismantle the Welfare State directed at those who got 'too big for their boots'), and it thrives because it is rooted in a philosphical outlook which, like it or not, gave birth to the modern world: the individualistic conception of society and history. This is a conception which, in my view, the Left, except for some forms of anarchism, has never come to terms with, and which must be taken into account by every social scheme whose goal is liberation, an ever greater degree of human emancipation (and if not of the individual, who else?). It is no coincidence if contract theories are springing up again and there is talk of a new 'social contract'. Modern contract theory grows out of the inversion of the holistic and organic conception of society (the prevailing concept from Aristotle to Hegel according to which the whole is greater than the sum of its parts), that is to say it grew out of the idea that the starting point for every social scheme for human emancipation is the individual with *passions* (to be channelled or tamed), *interests* (to be regulated and co-ordinated), and *needs* (to be satisfied or repressed). The hypothesis from which modern contract theory proceeds is the state of nature, a state in which there are only isolated individuals but ones predisposed to join together to form a society so as to safeguard their own lives and freedom. Proceeding from this premiss political society becomes an artificial entity, a joint undertaking, the plans for which need to be constantly formulated and reformulated, a project which is never definitive, but needs to undergo continuous revision. The topicality of this new contractarianism also stems from the fact that polyarchic societies, which is what the societies we now inhabit have become by being simultaneously capitalist and democratic, are societies in which the bulk of collective decisions are arrived at via negotiations which finish in agreements, in other words where the social contract is no longer a rational hypothesis but a practical instrument of government in everyday use.

But which social contract? A social contract which allows contracting individuals to ask political society and hence the government, which is its natural expression, only for protection, which is historically what contractarians asked for, and what the new generation of liberal writers are asking for once more (Nozick's book is a good case in point)?[24] Or should there be instead a new social contract, in which what is at the centre of negotiations is some principle of distributive justice?[25] For some years now there has been prolonged debate on just this point. The democratic Left cannot pass it over. The crux of this debate is to see whether, starting with the same incontestable individualist conception of society and using the same institutional structures, we are able to make a counter-proposal to the theory of social contract which neo-liberals want to put into operation, one which would include in its conditions a principle of distributive justice and which would hence be compatible with the theoretical and practical tradition of socialism. There is new talk, even within the inner sanctum of the Italian Socialist Party, of liberal socialism.[26] It is my considered opinion that the only way liberal socialism can be discussed without straying into abstractions or outright contradictions is to devise a new social contract. It is thus a subject of which a lot more will be heard.

# 6

# Contract and Contractarianism in the Current Debate

When Henry Summer Maine defined the transition from archaic societies to evolved societies as the transition from a society based on *status* to one based on *contractus*, he was essentially referring to the sphere of private law.[1] It was a period when the growth of a commercial society, defined by Spencer as the intervening stage between military societies and industrial societies, was opening up the prospect of an expansion of civil society at the expense of the state. In other words, the sphere of private relations, conceived as being between individuals on an equal footing, seemed to be growing at the expense of public relations, seen as unequal because based on the supremacy of one section of society over the other, a process tending towards a weakening, not to say the actual disappearance, of the state, the entity which historically had wielded an exclusive and irresistible power.

Not only has the state not disappeared, it has actually grown and extended its sphere of influence to the point of evoking the metaphor of the octopus with a thousand tentacles. Nevertheless the image of the contract (bringing with it a full retinue of related images which precede it, follow it, and replace it) has survived and is increasingly used by political theorists in their analysis of the real relationships that occur within the state. They refer to political exchange and, by analogy with a commercial transaction (a phenomenon symptomatic of the private sphere of relationships and always thought of as not only taking place outside the public sphere, but as actually antithetical to it), and also to the political market-place. They talk of an exchange vote, as opposed to the traditional opinion vote, as if the vote too were a commodity which is acquired by paying, or more realistically promising, the 'due equivalent of a price' (I am intentionally using the expression which Article 1420 of the Italian Civil Code uses in its definition of a contract of sale). This is a price which the politician (whom Schumpeter has for good reason equated with an entrepreneur), meets out of the public resources which he has, or believes he has, at his disposal. Then there is the more general nexus of relationships formed between larger interest groups or power groups which are a feature of the pluralist and polyarchical society which capitalist democracies have become and which exist over and above the personal or personalized relations obtaining between the political class and citizens, between the rulers and the ruled. Here too, in Italy and elsewhere, political scientists have evolved a terminology modelled on exchange relations as opposed to power relations, and talk of conflicts being resolved via bargaining, trans-actions, negotiations, compromises, settlements, agreements, and culminating, hopefully at least, in a 'social contract' when it concerns social conflict (the trade unions), or in a 'political contract' if it concerns political conflict (the political parties), or even in a 'national contract' when constitutional reform is involved. In Italian politics it is widely assumed that there exists a '*conventio ad excludendum*', an agreement (tacit, of course) between some parties not to let others into the government coalition. Some go so far as discussing the possibility of reformulating the constitutional basis of political consensus in this spirit, and do so in terms which are no longer descriptive but prescriptive, or to put it mildly, tendentious. They thus envisage a new type of social contract, and by doing so are resurrecting the old idea, which fell into discredit after the crisis of natural law theory brought about by the impact of historicism and utilitarianism, that political society should be conceived as having originated in a voluntary agreement between individuals who were, at least formally, equal.

### CRISIS OF THE SOVEREIGN STATE

Naturally it is important not to lump together things which are actually distinct, and I will come to some important qualifications to what I am saying later. But for the moment I simply want to point out that all the contractual terminology which is traditionally used to portray the sphere of private interests existing below the state's jurisdiction (and even the sphere of international relations which exists above it) suggests a conceptualization of the sphere of public law as situated in between the spheres of private law and inter-national law, something quite at variance with the way public law has actually been conceived in mainstream political and juridical theory ever since the state started to emerge in its modern form. I talk of 'conceptualization' because the central image underlying the theory of the modern state is of the *law*, rather than private agreement, as the essential source of norms governing interpersonal relations. In this respect it stands in marked contrast to the concept of contract, whose normative force is subordinated to that of the law, and which is only valid within limits defined by the law (contract only reappears in the form of treaty between equal sovereign states). Even where the state is held to come into being with an original agreement or pact, the object of this *pactum subiectionis* or *dominationis* (no different from Rousseau's social contract, which is also a 'pact of subjection', if not in form then in effect) is to confer on a human agent, whether natural (a king) or artificial (an assembly), the right to impose its own will via that norm binding on the whole community, which we call the law. The contracting parties to this pact may be the people on one side and the sovereign on the other (thus involving a bilateral contract), or alternatively individuals can agree among themselves to obey a sovereign body (thus involving a multilateral contract, or what might be better termed a collective act). In both cases, the image of the contract serves as the basis of a system of coexistence whose principal source of right, and hence of the regulation of social relations, will, once the constituting role of the original contract is complete, no longer be the contract or agreement between equals, but the law which institutes relations of subordination. The power which makes a sovereign a sovereign, which turns a society, made up of parts in mutable and ephemeral relations to each other, into a state, a unified dominion or totality, is legislative power. The idea of the political community, from the Greek *polis* to the modern state, is inextricably bound up with the idea of a totality which, in contrast to the state of nature, unifies parts which would otherwise remain in perpetual conflict with each other. What guarantees the unity of the whole is law, and the power to make the laws, *condere leges*, belongs to the sovereign.

But we are dealing with an 'image'. The reality of political life is very different. Political life proceeds through a series of conflicts which are never definitely resolved, and whose temporary resolution comes about through provisional agreements, truces, and those more durable peace treaties called constitutions. This contrast between image and reality is well illustrated by the way the traditional conflict between social classes and the monarch, between parliament and the crown continue unabated throughout modern history, while in the very same period the doctrine of the state was being formulated in the works of political writers and theorists of public law, from Bodin to Rousseau, from Hobbes to Hegel, all of which hinge on the concepts of sovereignty, the unity of power and the primacy of legislative power. But such political doctrines always have a normative as well as an expositional function, for, even if they like to present themselves as a way of understanding and explaining what actually happens, they are also blueprints of what ought to be. As such they sometimes substitute themselves for reality, forcing it, adapting it, simplifying it to reduce it to a neat, unified and coherent system. Since the driving force behind a political doctrine is not only intellectual passion but a visionary urge to change reality, it can have the effect of delaying the realization that major changes are taking place or of providing distorted interpretations of what these changes are. One of the features of the doctrine of the state which still prevails happens to be the primacy of public law, and as a result it is held to be impossible for situations covered by public law to be understood in terms of the traditional categories of private law.

A good example of this position is provided by Hegel, who maintained that the major categories of private law, property and contract, are inadequate to comprehend the reality of public law, for this governs the organization of the whole, while private law is concerned with the resolution of conflicts between parties who are at least formally equal, and who remain independent notwithstanding juridical constraints . Nor does he see them providing a convincing justification of the majesty of the state, which has power of life and death over its citizens, and which citizens are not free to leave, like they can any other society (even the family once they have come of age). Nor can these categories act as a solid foundation for political philosophy, for this deals not with 'a world of atomic particles' but with an organic whole, in which every part is a function of every other and all are a function of the totality.[2] According to this conception of the relationship between private and public law, a society where political relations are all subsumed within the category of private law, as in the Middle Ages, epitomizes an age of decadence. Hence for Hegel, the Holy Roman Empire is no longer a state because the relationship between the princes and the empire and the princes and each other, which ought to be regulated by public law, are in fact treated as if they were relationships of private law (family and property relations).

### 'PARTICULARISM' AS A HISTORICAL CATEGORY

I have made this reference to the Middle Ages with a specific point in mind. When it started to become apparent, especially after the First

World War, that there was a significant gap between the traditional model of the state as a concentrated, homogenous and organic power and the reality of a fragmented society divided into hostile factions tending to fight each other for ascendancy and establish truces rather than durable peace settlements, it became common to talk nostalgically of a return to the Middle Ages. At least it did among political journalists of a right-wing orientation, ill-equipped by prevailing doctrines of the state to appreciate that what seemed a degenerative phase in the formation of the modern state was really a situation which was normal, or was to become normal, in modern democracies, the only alternative to which could be authoritarian regimes (as in fact proved to be the case then and is just as true today). But in order to understand that discord was bound to remain the normal state of affairs, it was necessary not to be mesmerized by the prevailing doctrine, which made a rigid distinction between public and private law, and had looked on the inexorable trend towards pluralism with suspicion. Followers of this doctrine saw this period of social development, when the number of active citizens increased, thanks to universal suffrage, and the growth of increasingly powerful trade unions and mass parties had multiplied the reasons for conflict and intensified its consequences, as a regression away from the triumphal march towards the supra-individual collective state, uniform and unifying. This attitude of anxiety and concern at these pluralistic forces eventually found expression in the withering critiques of democracy formulated by authors as different as Pareto and Carl Schmitt.

The temptations to react in this way are just as strong today: one of the striking features of contemporary political commentators, from whatever ideological wavelength of the parliamentary spectrum, is the continual lament at the way individual interests persist in making their presence felt and the denunciation of 'particularism' (the category 'particularism', together with its concrete manifestations 'guild' and 'faction', has had negative connotations throughout the entire history of political thought). The corollary of this is the constant assertion of the superiority of the collective or national interest, which in any case people are incapable of defining precisely, except by interpreting it as the interest of their own social group. Last but not least there is the claim that if particular interests are given priority over general ones, the 'private' over the 'public', the state, still conceived in terms of the conventional doctrine, ceases to be a totality in which everything is subsumed, but becomes instead a conglomeration of parts piled up in a heap (the metaphor of the pile of stones to represent the antithesis of an organic whole comes from

Hegel). Admittedly if we look closely, the social and political reality which confronts us every day is so multifarious and multifaceted, and hence so impossible to fit into models based on public law inherited from the doctrine of the state of the last few centuries from Bodin to Weber and right up to Kelsen, as to make it perfectly understandable that people take refuge in a state of mind situated somewhere between the *laudatio temporis acti*, a nostalgia for a time which never existed, and the longing for a restoration (likely to be impossible except at the price of throwing away the baby of democracy with the bath-water of particularism, a baby which still has to grow and whose fate is either to grow up with pluralism or to die). A well-known French academic, having given a description of modern society as divided, disjointed, fragmented, incapable of rediscovering the unity it has lost (the exact opposite of the 'mono-lithic society' that some others characterize it as, which shows how profoundly mysterious our increasingly complex societies have become), coined a word for this state of affairs. He called it a 'mérécracie', a 'cracy' of parts (one of the many pejorative 'cracies' with which political terminology abounds).[3] Besides, what is the widely used Italian term 'partyocracy', invented by Giuseppe Maranini at the time when the practice of party wheeling and dealing in Italy was starting to come in for criticism, if not an equivalent, less erudite but more incisive polemically, of 'merecracy'? What does 'partyocracy' mean if not the overpowering of the whole by its parts, in other words the contemporary form taken by the eternal force of particularism?

But jeremiads are far from being an analysis and even less do they constitute a diagnosis. The formal constitution is one thing, the real constitution, or material constitution as jurists would say, is quite another, and it is the latter which has to be reckoned with. According to the famous remark of a great American lawyer, law is made by lawyers. Paraphrasing this, we might say that constitutions are made by political forces: they make them when they give rise to them in the first place, they make and remake them freely when they put them into practice (much more freely than judges are able to when applying the law). In a democratic society the political forces are organized parties: organized primarily to obtain votes, to procure as many as possible. It is they who woo the public to obtain its consent. On them depends the greater or lesser degree of legitimation that prevails in the political system at a given time. Article 49 of the Italian Constitution, to which great importance is attached, confines itself to the statement that political parties are legally permitted:[4] a completely superfluous clause, because, despite the rivers of ink that have flowed to substantiate this provision, parties are much more than permissible. They are necessary: and it is here that their strength lies.

## THE MACROPOLITICAL MARKET-PLACE

Where there is more than on party, which is the *conditio sine qua non* of democracy, and especially when there are many of them, as in Italy, the logic which governs their dealings with each other is the logic of the agreement under private law, and not the logic of a power relationship as under public law. There is no trace of this contractual logic in the Italian constitution: the constitution deals with the way laws are formed, but the formation of agreements (bilateral or multilateral contracts) is covered by the civil code. Yet it is impossible to understand anything about the way a constitution moves, shifts and is slowly altered unless one is aware of the dense mesh of agreements underlying the coalitions between parties and what factions are excluded from them. In the Constitutional Charter the formation of government (Articles 92 onwards) is defined as the result of a series of unilateral acts typical of a power relationship: the President of the Republic appoints the President of the Council;[5] he in turn chooses the ministers and forwards their names to the President of the Republic; the government assumes office when the two chambers formally entrust it with power, it falls when this trust is withdrawn in a vote of no confidence. This sequence of unilateral acts of authority conceals the reality of what is going on behind the scenes, namely a series of deals, arrangements and agreements laboriously arrived at, whose binding force depends, as is true of all agreements, on respect for the principle of *do ut des*. A government can fall because a party secretary withdraws his ministers from a coalition, an act which, if judged in terms of the constitutional norms officially regulating the life of a government, would be an aberration. It only ceases to be aberrant when it is judged from the point of view of the written and unwritten norms which apply to any agreement, the basic one being that an agreement is liable to be revoked when one of the parties does not fulfill the obligations he has undertaken. Had or had not one of the parties undertaken to approve a certain parliamentary bill? If so, and he subsequently did not approve it, or approved it in a manner which had not itself been approved, the agreement is off, and the other party is perfectly within his rights to cancel it unilaterally. Critics can shout out scandal until they are blue in the face: outside observers who want to understand what is going on must confine themselves to recognizing the fact that a fundamental principle of democratic public law, which decrees that a government stays in office till it is overthrown by a majority decision, has given way to a principle which is just as fundamental to private law, which lays down that agreements must be honoured. When a crisis breaks out involving the formation of a new government, it is customary to invoke the notorious Article 92, paragraph 2, which stipulates that the choice of ministers to be submitted to the President of the Council is the responsiblity of the designated President of the Republic. It has never been possible to apply this norm because the distribution of the various ministries among the different parties and even within the same party, and even who is going to be appointed to specific ministries, is all arranged in advance via agreements between the parties, which once again prove themselves to be stronger than the constitution itself. According to the hierachical relationship which is supposed to exist between the various sources of law, it is a fundamental principle that contracts must comply with what is established by law (though this concerns contracts made within private law). In this case the reverse is happening: the power of the President of the Council is exercised within the limits imposed on it by agreements between the parties, so much so that someone once defined the Manuale Cencelli, or Cencelli manual, as the basis of the Italian constitution.[6]

It is true that unlike private agreements and even international agreements, political agreements are informal, in that they are not regulated by law. But anyone who had the patience to assemble empirical data on the way the coalition government of a country like Italy actually functions, based as is it on a general pact to exclude certain parties from power and on an enormous number of alliances involving two, three, four or any number of parties, could perhaps write a handbook of constitutional law of contract to stand alongside the private and the international law of contract, something that to my knowledge nobody has so far attempted. What such an exercise would reveal, among other things, is that many of the norms which are already codified in the law of contract (or international treaties) apply equally to the formulation, alteration and cancellation of political agreements, ranging from the norms concerning basic conditions, to the general principle, almost a natural law, that agreements must be entered into in good faith, from the general rules covering the vices of consensus to the various grounds for annulling a contractual agreement.

The case of the binding mandate is the most illuminating example of the gap between the constitution in theory and practice, because of the light it throws on how particularism has gained ascendancy over the principle of organic unity. Although the veto on the binding mandate has always been considered one of the cardinal provisions of representative democracy ever since the American and French Revolutions, it is in practice inoperable.[7] The idea that representatives, by virtue of being elected, become members of the sovereign body of a democratic state, parliament, and thereby must exercise their mandate freely, unconstrained by the demands of their electors, which can only be demands made in order to satisfy individual or corporate interests, is one of the most characteristic arguments used by writers in political theory and public law. They adopt this thesis to defend the integrity of state power (whose guarantee is the sovereign, whether a monarch or the people) against the particularism of vested interests. There are two ways of representing electors: either by mandation, where representatives are like delegates and confine themselves to transmitting the demands made by those they represent, or by representation, whereby once elected representatives are no longer bound by the wishes of their electors who only form a part of the whole, and are free to judge what interests are to be safeguarded. They do so on the assumption that the electors, *uti singuli*, have given them the mandate to look after collective interests and on the premiss that individual interests must be subordinated to the collective interest. The passage from mandation to representation can be interpreted as the transition from a conception of the mandatary based on private law, according to which mandatories act in the name and on behalf of the mandator, and if they do not act within the limits of the mandate can be recalled, to a conception based on public law according to which the relationship between elector and elected representative can no longer be conceived as a contractual agreement, because both parties are invested with a public function and their relationship is typical of a ceremony of investiture, whereby the power conferred on the person taking public office is to be exercised in the public interest.

But nowadays anyone who reflects realistically on how decisions are taken in a parliament – where deputies or MPs have to toe the party line (and if they refuse it is not always to defend national interests against vested interests but because they are falling in with wishes of pressure groups, which in some respects represent interests even more particular than those of the parties) must admit that a solemn statement like the one made in Article 67 of the Constitution, that 'Every member of parliament represents the Nation', sounds hollow, if not actually ridiculous. Every member of parliament represents first and foremost his own party, just as in a nation consisting of estates, the delegates represented primarily the interests of their own estates. By saying this I do not want to draw an anachronistic parallel between the 'estates of the realm' of early modern times and contemporary political parties, but simply to highlight how difficult it is to apply the ideal of the state which transcends its parts, even when political subjects are no longer groups, estates, or orders which defend their particular interests, but individuals in a democracy entrusted with a public function. The difficulty derives from the fact that the sub-groups which Rousseau understandably wanted to banish from his republic, because they put sectional interests first, not only have not disappeared with the advent of democracy, but have enormously increased, as a result both of the development of democracy itself, which gave rise to mass parties, and because of the emergence of large-scale organizations for the defence of economic interests within industrial societies, bodies which are characterized by a concentration of economic power. The continuous negotiations carried out between these quasi-sovereign power elites constitute the real web of power relations in contemporary society, in which government, the 'sovereign' in the traditional sense of the word, and as such supposed to be placed *super partes*, is just one power elite among others and not necessarily the strongest one at that.

## THE MICROPOLITICAL MARKET-PLACE

If the bargaining between parties constitutes the macropolitical market, the bargaining between the parties and citizens constitutes the micropolitical market, a political market *par excellence* through which citizens, invested with a public responsibility by virtue of their role as electors, become *clientes*. Once again a relationship of a public character is transformed into one of a private character. Moreover this form of privatization of what was initially public stems from a previous instance of the same phenomenon, considered earlier. Namely, the capacity of parties to keep a firm grip on their deputies and to maintain the promises candidates made to the electorate. The one follows on from the other in that the conversion of the elector into a client is only made possible by the conversion of the unrestricted mandate into a binding one. The two processes are inextricably bound up with each other and both are expressions of the dissolution of the organic unity of the state which formed the essential core of the theory and ideology of the modern state (more an ideology than a theory). At the same time, they are a corruption of the principle of individualism from which modern democracy originated, whose ground rule is the rule of the majority based on the principle of one man (or woman) one vote.

There is no doubt that modern democracy originated from the individualistic, atomistic conception of society (how individualism itself was born is another problem more difficult to resolve because the aspirants to the role of founder are many and varied). Nor is it in doubt that representative democracy originates from the premiss (albeit erroneous) that individuals, once entrusted with the public function of choosing their representatives, would choose the 'best'. There is a passage in a letter by Madison published in *The Federalist*, which always causes great mirth when I read it to my students. It is the passage where he says that one of the advantages of representative democracy consists in the election of a 'chosen body of citizens, whose wisdom may best discern the true interest of their country, and whose patriotism and love of justice, will be least likely to sacrifice it to temporary or partial considerations'.[8] The premiss is mistaken, because it is impossible to imagine why, when citizens are called upon to choose a representatives, they would not opt for the person or group which offered the best guarantee of protecting their interests. Despite the durability of this illusion it is difficult to understand how people could ever convince themselves that it would be otherwise. The old definition of membership of a party as *idem sentire de re publica*, encouraged the misguided belief that whoever votes for a party does so because he is convinced of the soundness of the ideas which it stands for, what we would nowadays call an opinion vote. In a mass society opinion votes are becoming increasingly few and far between: I would go so far as to say that the only genuine opinion in modern elections is the one held by those who do not vote because they have come to realize, or so they think, that elections are a ritual that can be opted out of without causing serious damage, and which like all rituals, such as going to church on a Sunday, are, when it comes down to it, just a drag. This opinion may be debatable, reprehensible, despicable, but it is an opinion nonetheless. In contrast, the exchange vote is on the increase as the voters get more sly and the parties more shrewd. One cannot explain otherwise the process we see taking place before our very eyes in a multi-party system such as the Italian: namely the transformation or degradation of small parties such as the Social Democrats into simple pressure groups (representing the pensioners, for example), or of the larger composite parties, such as the Christain Democrats, into a collection of different pressure groups and lobbies. When consent is traded for public resources, which is the peculiarity of a political contract, the interest of the electorate and the interest of the party coincide. The strength of a party is measured in the number of votes it obtains. The larger the number of votes bartered in the mini-market created between the party and the electorate, the greater the bargaining power of the party in the hypermarket created by the parties' dealings with each other. However in this larger market what counts is not only the number of votes that a party can put on the scales but its strategic place within the system of alliances. Thus a small party which plays a decisive role in forming a majority has greater specific weight, especially when, like the Italian Socialist Party, it not only holds the balance of power in the right-wing alliances at national level but in many cases in the left-wing alliances at regional level as well.

## THE POLITICAL MARKET-PLACE AND DEMOCRACY

Like it or not, the political market, meant in the specific sense that the principle of exchange dominates the relationship between rulers and the ruled, is a fundamental feature of democracy. Certainly not of the imaginary democracy of Rousseau and of all those who believe the increase in participation is in itself a panacea for all our ills (the participation of controllers, maybe, but not the participation of controllers who themselves are controlled), but of actually existing democracy which feeds off this constant exchange between producers and consumers (and conversely between consumers and producers of power). In a word, to have power means having the ability to reward or punish, i.e. to obtain from others the desired behaviour, either by making promises which can actually be fulfilled (rewards), or by making threats that can actually be carried out (punishments). In traditional societies, in which most people are subservient, count for nothing, and cannot intervene in the process of legitimation, the exercise of punitive power suffices to keep the vast majority ignorant, poor and deprived of civil, let alone political, rights. In a democracy this is not so. In a democracy the vast majority of citizens intervene actively in the process by which the system as a whole is legitimated by exercising their own right to vote and so upholding the constitution and the parties that embody it – and even by not using it, because in this case the principle that 'silence means consent' applies (no one has yet considered the manifestation of political apathy as a serious threat to democracies). Most importantly, they intervene in the allocation of the power to govern between the various competing political forces by the way they distribute their votes. As is natural, in a democratic system power cannot be maintained simply by using the stick. The carrot is equally necessary (a type of bargain). Leaving metaphors aside, expressing consent through the ballot box is an active way of doing someone a good turn. One good turn deserves another. A reciprocal readiness to do something in exchange for something else is the basis of bilateral contracts. The political market in a democratic state is made up of as many bilateral agreements as there are electors. In these agreements what is offered by the electorate is the vote, what the elected representative offers in return is an advantage (in the form of a benefit or a service) or else relief from a burden.

Lawyers distinguish between bilateral and multilateral contracts. The agreements in the smaller political market fit into the first category, while those in the greater one between politicians belong to the second. In the case of the first, the two parties each have a distinctive role (which is given a specific name): buyer/seller, lessee/lessor, depositor/depository, lender/borrower, and, in the context of political exchange, representative/represented. In the second category all parties have the same role, that of partners. In the first the two parties have different objectives but a common interest, which is to effect an exchange, while in the second the various parties have different interests but a common objective, namely the one for which the society was constituted. While in the case of the agreement constitutive of political exchange, the undertakings of the two parties are relatively clear (protection in return for consent), the agreements made in the greater market, which give rise to government coalitions (opposition coalitions are more rare), have a common objective which is in general terms to form a government and to govern, but in more specific terms is so varied and complex that it is difficult and even pointless to try to decide what it is. At most it is possible to distinguish genuine government agreements (as with provisions relating to a particular set of questions concerning the economy, society or public order and constituting the programme of the government) from agreements at a subgovernmental level which concern the equitable distribution of responsibilities and posts. Precisely because of the variety and vastness of the issues which can be covered by such agreements, they are liable at any moment to break down and to be unilaterally annulled, or to be revised and reformulated by common consent, especially when, as in the Italian political system, the partners are as quarrelsome as they are numerous. Moreover, because of the intimate link noted earlier between the relationship within the different factions and the relationship which each faction has to maintain with its own clients, none of the partners can afford not to monitor constantly the moods of the clientele, for, as we have said, their bargaining power directly depends on the greater or lesser support it gives them. The validity of an agreement not regulated by a legal norm emanating from an authority higher than the contracting parties is governed by the principle *rebus sic stantibus*. Among the mutable *res* which can cause one of the parties to back out of an agreement are the warning signs which come from below.

The difference between the relationship that is established between electors and those they elect, and the one between the various political factions, is also manifested in the two different skills that good politicians must have: in the first they behave as an entrepreneur, while in the second they are more of a negotiator. In Italy the gifts of a good entrepreneur are essential for a party secretary, while those of a negotiator are needed by the President of the Council.

### THE REVIVAL OF CONTRACTARIANSIM

We must now turn to consider the third way that insights into the nature of contract can throw light on the dynamics of the contemporary state and the political phenomena associated with it. These are connected with social contract theories, or so-called 'contractarianism'. There is certainly renewed interest in the contractarian theories of the past, so much so that it does not seem inappropriate to talk of a 'neo-contractarianism'. This interest is due in part to the success of Rawls's book on justice which actually takes as its starting-point the 'familiar theory of the social contract as found, say in Locke, Rousseau and Kant' to expound his theory of justice.[9] In actual fact Rawls's theory of justice, even if it has a contractarian basis in taking as its premiss an original contract between rational individuals, has very little to do with social contract theories, the aim of which was to justify rationally the existence of the state, to find a rational foundation of political power and of the maximum power of man over man and not to propose a model of the just society. The central problem which occupied the theorists of *ius naturale*, who include (apart from those cited by Rawls) Hobbes, Spinoza, Pufendorf and many others, was never justice, but power, and in particular the power which has no other power placed above it: sovereign power. With regard to this power of life and death based in the last resort on the exclusive right to use force, the basic question which political philosophers have always asked themselves is what justification can such a power have. Contractarianism is just one of the possible answers to this question: hence the problem it set itself to resolve was the problem of the legitimacy of power and not that of justice as such.

The deeper reason for the revival of interest in contractarianism resides in the fact that the notion of an original contract to lay the foundation of society as a whole, as distinct from the partial societies which eventually compose it, satisfies the need for a sense of beginning, or rather of a new beginning, in an age of profound upheavals within existing society. What springs to mind to illustrate this is Sieyès's exhortation to the Third Estate to declare itself a National Assembly and act as if it was leaving the state of nature and was called upon to form the Social Contract.[10]

In contrast, one of the reasons for the eclipse of contractarian theories between the end of the seventeenth century and the end of the eighteenth, was the influence of the idea that the state was too sublime an entity to be explained as the artificial product of an accord between individuals. It is well known how much Hegel's anti-contractarianism owes to this argument. But no less revealing is this passage from Burke (significantly a political writer who was a realist, a traditionalist, hostile to the Enlightenment and considered one of the fathers of modern historicism):

> Society is indeed a contract. Subordinate contracts for objects of mere occasional interest may be dissolved at pleasure – but the state ought not to be considered as nothing better than a partnership agreement in a trade of pepper, and coffee, calico or tobacco, or some other such low concern, to be taken up for a little temporary interest and to be dissolved by the fancies of the parties. It should be looked on with other reverence.[11]

What helped to give the *coup de grâce* to contractarian theories, apart from orthodox philosophical and historical arguments according to which the original contract was a 'chimera', were two somewhat more debatable historical interpretations: the portrayal of the Middle Ages as a society in which political relations were supposed to be equally of a contractual kind, and the celebrated Marxian critique according to which Rousseau's social contract, which establishes via a pact a relationship between individuals who are by nature independent, is the rationalization of the bourgeois society which had been emerging since the sixteenth society.[12] The reference to the Middle Ages as a society based on contract is a fallacy: when we read, to quote an authoritative text, that the obligations of reciprocity between king and bishops, between king and the first of the realm are the equivalent of a *pactum*,[13] this contractarian interpretation of the power relations has nothing to do with the problem of an original social contract, for this act is not a bilateral contract but is a collective act, which it is a misnomer to call 'contract'. As for the Marxian interpretation, this is an unwarranted generalization from a warranted historical observation: even if contractarianism originated with the growth of the bourgeois world (but how much vagueness there is in this over-used and abused expression!), the individualistic conception of society which under-lies modern democracy is no more bourgeois than it is proletarian. In fact it is more proletarian than it is bourgeois, for the simple reason that while no bourgeois government would have gone, of its own accord, beyond a suffrage resticted only to property owners, the extension of the suffrage to include the have-nots only came about thanks to pressure from below exerted by the working-class movement. And universal suffrage is the necessary, if not sufficient, condition for the existence and smooth working of a democratic system, in so far as it is the fruit of the fundamental principle of democracy, that the source of power is individuals *uti singuli*, with every individual counting equally (which among other things is the justification of majority rule in taking collective decisions). To consider the state as founded on a social contract, i.e on a common accord of all those who will henceforth be subject to it, means defending the cause of ascending as against descending power, means upholding the principle that power moves up from bottom to top and not down from top to bottom: in a word it means establishing democracy to counteract autocracy. The image of the social contract is not to be confused with the power relations of medieval society, even when they are redefined as contractual relations: the latter are in fact bilateral relations, based on reciprocity, and thus have nothing to do with the idea of ascending power which is expressed in the social contract. Thus, when the subject of the contract is linked to the theme of bourgeois commercial society, the contract being referred to (and it is precisely the one Marx refers to in some famous passages) is here too one of the typical forms of agreement between two formally equal parties, like the one established between the buyer and seller of the labour force, a type of agreement which once again has nothing to do with the multilateral agreement or collective act which is at the basis of the social contract.

Because the theory of the social contract hinges on rational arguments and is bound up with the birth of democracy (even if not all contractarian theories are democratic) it has never been totally eclipsed. There were even contractarian theories in the last century, and in every case the champions of the social contract defended it by appealing to the principle of the individual as the ultimate source of the power to wield authority over the self-same individuals, thus rejecting the traditional conceptions of the state which were suprapersonal, organic, collectivist, holistic, universalistic. In a book written at the end of the nineteenth century but which I have never seen quoted in recent debates, *Contrattualismo e sociologia contemporanea* (*Contractarianism and Contemporary Sociology*), the author Salvatore Fragapane, a philosopher of law who died at an early age, carried out a critical analysis of such contractarian thought as had, along with individualism, survived the headstrong advance of sociology pioneered by Comte and which had dismissed the individualistic premiss as a metaphysical abstraction, repugnant to positive science. Fragapane refers to the growing 'contractualization' of individual relations, already remarked on by Maine and Spencer, which leads him to a penetrating observation, which not only has lost none of its relevance, but is if anything more relevant than ever: 'both industrialism, with its need for capitalist forces on a large scale which can only be provided by powerful associations, and the division of labour, with its continuous tendency to break down into smaller units, and for exchanges hence to become increasingly specific, necessitate the use of contractual arrangements, not only in the commercial and civil sphere of relations, *but in the political sphere as well.*'[14] Yet at the same time he correctly underlines the difference between this phenomenon of the contractualization of socio-economic relations, which positivist social science is bound to acknowledge as an empirical fact, and the traditional theory of the original contract. For the former 'is not the expression of an act of free will taking place in a vacuum at the origins of the social phenomenon ... but rather a higher phase of social development; it is not the arbitrary act of an individual, but a collective wish manifesting a law peculiar to a particular phase of social evolution.'[15]

What does not emerge clearly enough from this distinction between an original 'metaphysical' contract and the phenomenon of the contractualization of society, is that while the second is the object of historical analysis, the first is a normative model, which is neither confirmed nor refuted by the second, because it exists on a completely different plane. However, when nowadays we talk of neo-contractarianism in reference to social contract theories, it should be clear that, just as Fragapane had pointed out, the problem of reshaping the foundations of society on the basis of the contractarian model of society is quite another issue from the problem posed by the fragmentation of central power into a host of lesser and generally antagonistic powers, leading to the emergence of what are called in

Italian 'partial governments' (*governi parziali*), and thus to dealings between them which are naturally of a contractual nature. One could almost be tempted to say that the first derives from the need to find a solution to the second.

## THE NEW ALLIANCES

Let me make my position clear. A basic feature of an agreement based on a bargaining relationship between two parties who consider themselves mutually independent is that it is by its very nature unstable, and prone to make the whole social structure unstable. As proof of this it is enough to think of the volatile nature of the international community. Contracts based on private law prosper, and promote social development, under the protection of the coercive force of the state which guarantees that they will be honoured in a social entity where, despite the growing 'corporatization' of society and the growth of increasingly powerful economic groupings, the state has still retained and sustained the monopoly of force. This does not happen in the international community, in which the free competition of force still prevails, even if on a reduced scale. It is even less true of the relations between the power centres which exist within the state, over which the state still formally retains the monopoly of force, but which it cannot exercise effectively, and in fact is extremely wary of exercising. This thesis is proved by the reluctance with which a government intervenes to get a public service back working properly in the case of a strike which is illegal, or manifestly against the public interest of which it is supposed to be the representative and the guarantor. (There was a case in Italy when a judge, the traditional and archetypal embodiment of the coercive power of the state, intervened in a labour dispute, upon which the two parties responsible for the negotiations expressed the most indignant protests!) The impotence of the state, when confronted with controversies between the powerful interest groups that have taken up positions within it, is reminiscent of the impotence of the United Nations when faced by controversies between states, even if formally the state has the monopoly of legitimate force while the international organization does not. But what is legitimacy without the means of making it effective? Certainly there will always be an important difference between having the monopoly of power without being able to exercise it, on the one hand, and not having it at all in the first place on the other. But it is surprising, almost paradoxical, that while people are calling for a strengthening of the state's power to influence dealings between nations, we are witnessing a steady weakening of the state's power within individual nations, except in those states where military power has gained the upper hand over political power.

Neo-contractarianism, i.e. the call for a new social contract, all-embracing not piecemeal, to create general harmony and found a new social order, a genuine 'new alliance', stems from a recognition of the chronic weakness which the power of the state displays in the most economically and politically advanced societies, or, to use the current phrase, from the growing ungovernability of complex societies. If anything, the greatest difficulty which neo-contractarianism has to face today derives from the fact that individuals retain, all independently of each other, a small portion of sovereign power, and are thus protagonists of the continuous process of legitimation and relegitimation of the bodies charged with taking collective decisions. Hence it is they who in the last analysis have the right to determine the terms of such a new social contract, and are no longer content to ask in return for their obedience simply the protection of their fundamental rights and of the property they have acquired through commercial activity (which is Nozick's theory of the minimal state). Instead they also ask for some clause to be inserted in the pact which ensures an equal distribution of wealth so as to diminish, if not eliminate, the inequalities between the positions which people start out from in life (which explains the success of Rawls's book, which sets out precisely to devise a way of meeting this demand). This call for equality is so deep-rooted and widespread that it has now moved from the national to the international level. It is hardly necessary to remind the reader that the great innovation introduced by the United Nations, which sets it apart from the League of Nations, consisted in the setting up of the Economic and Social Council. This body launched a programme of aid for developing countries and made sure that the agenda of debates between nations was no longer concerned solely with international *order* but also international *justice*. This innovation is symbolized by the way talk of the East-West divide, which perpetuates, even if on a large scale, the traditional problem of order, has now had superimposed on it talk of a North-South divide, which raises the totally new issue of a form of justice existing not only between classes or social groups within states but between states. Such a project faces enormous obstacles, because attempts to realize the vision of an international Welfare State on a colossal scale have to contend with the fact that the project to create a Welfare State even within individual nations has only been partially realized, and is now experiencing a severe crisis.

If and how such a vision might be realized no one, I believe, is in a position to say. What no one can doubt is that the solution of this problem is the awesome historical challenge which the Left is called upon to meet in a world which is ravaged by the forces of destruction.

# 7

# The Rule of Men or the Rule of Law

The nagging question that recurs throughout the history of political thought is: 'What is the better form of government, the one based on the rule of men or on the rule of law?'[1] The changing responses to this question forms one of the most significant and fascinating chapters in the evolution of political philosophy.

At the outset we must be on our guard against confusing this question with the equally traditional one of what constitutes the best form of government. Ever since the famous argument between three Persian princes narrated by Herodotus about whether rule by one, a few or many is best, the debate about the optimum form of government has always centred on the comparison between the virtues and defects of monarchy, aristocracy and democracy respectively, and sometimes on the possibility of resolving the differences with a form of government which incorporates elements of all three, so-called mixed government. This argument adopts as its yardstick of assessment and choice the number of those who rule. But each of them has a negative counterpart: for monarchy there is tyranny, for aristocracy oligarchy, and for democracy ochlocracy or mob-rule. This implies that any attempt to form a judgement on the best form of government mut take into account not only who the rulers are and how many of them, but also how they govern. The alternative question, 'the rule of men or of law?', concerns the second problem, not the *form* of government, but the *way* government operates. In other words it raises another issue, and proceeds within the framework of another distinction, namely between good and bad government.[2] In fact it can be rephrased in another way: 'Is good government one where the rulers are good because they govern in accordance with the established laws, or one where the laws are good because the rulers are wise?'

In support of the primacy of the rule of law over the rule of men two authoritative texts have come down to us from the Greeks, one by Plato and one by Aristotle. The first is Plato's *Laws*:

> If I have called them 'servants of the laws' it's not because I want to mint a new expression but because I believe that the success or failure of a state hinges on this point more that anything else. Where the law is subject to some other authority and has none of its own, the collapse of the state is not far off; but if the law is the master of the government and the government is its slave, then the situation is full of promise and men enjoy all the blessings that the gods shower on a state.[3]

The second is from Aristotle's *Politics*:

> We begin by asking whether it is more expedient to be ruled by the best man or by the best laws. Those who believe that to be ruled by a king is expedient think that the laws enunciate only general principles and do not give day-to-day instructions on matters as they arise; and so, they argue, in any skill it is foolish to be guided always by written laws ... On the other hand, rulers cannot do without that general principle in addition: it provides something which by its nature does not feel. Every human soul must have feelings, whereas a law has none.[4]

The main argument in favour of the thesis which opposes the notion of the superiority of the rule of men over the rule of law appears in the criticism which Aristotle makes of royal power in this passage. The criticism is clearly directed at the position Plato takes in *The Statesman*. This Platonic dialogue sets out to establish the nature of the 'royal science', in other words the form of scientific knowledge which enables anyone in its possession to govern well. Having asserted that one component of the royal science is legislative science, the Stranger comes out with this quip: 'Yet the best thing of all is not that the law should rule, but that a man should rule supposing him to have wisdom and royal power.' When Socrates asks why, the other replies: 'Because the law does not perfectly comprehend what is noblest and most just for all and therefore cannot enforce what is best'. Immediately afterwards he takes the argument to extremes by maintaining that any law which claims to apply to all cases at all times is 'like an obstinate and ignorant tyrant, who will not allow anything to be done contrary to his appointment, or any question to be asked'.[5] There follows the usual parable to illustrate the point:

> As the pilot watches over the interests of this ship and of the crew – not by laying down rules, but by making his art a law – preserves the lives of his fellow-sailors, even so, and in the salf-same way, may there not be a true form of polity created by those who are able to govern in a similar spirit, and who show a strength or art which is superior to the law?[6]

As one can see, whoever asserts the superiority of the rule of men turns his opponent's argument completely on its head. The very feature of law which for the latter constitutes its postive virtue, namely its 'generality', becomes for the former its basic drawback, precisely because law cannot take account of all possible cases and therefore needs the intervention of an enlightened ruler if all are is to be given their just desserts. Yet someone could defend the opposing point of view by invoking a second feature of law: the fact that it is 'dispassionate'. What Aristotle wants to convey with this phrase is that where the ruler respects the law he cannot allow his personal preferences to influence his decisions. In other words, respect for the law guarantees the impartiality of the ruler by preventing him from exercising his power to pursue his own interests, just as the rules of medical practice, applied properly, prevent doctors from treating their patients differently according to whether they are friends or enemies. While the primacy of the law protects the citizen from the arbitrary use of power by the bad ruler, the primacy of people protects him from the indiscriminateness of a general norm, that is as long as the ruler is good. The first solution shields the individual from the arbitrariness of decisions, the second from the excessively general nature of the legal precepts underlying them. Just as the second presupposes a good ruler, so the premiss of the first assumes good laws. The two solutions are presented as polar opposites of each other, as if an absolute choice was involved: either/or. In actual fact both of them presuppose a condition which, as the conditions change, render them interchangeable. The primacy of the law is based on the premiss that rulers are mostly bad, in the sense that they tend to use power for their own ends. The primacy of those in office is based on the opposite premiss of the good ruler, whom classical thinkers conceived as the great legislator. In fact, if rulers are wise what need is there for them to be constrained by a network of general laws which prevent him from weighing up the pros and cons of each case? Certainly, but if the ruler is bad is it not preferable for him to be subject to general norms which prevent anyone holding power from making their own caprice the criterion for judging what is just and unjust?

If the alternatives are presented in these terms, and their real implications are explained in these terms, there is no getting away from the fact that down the centuries the choice has been made overwhelmingly in favour of the rule of law and there has been, generally speaking, a negative verdict on those whom fortune or virtue or a combination of both (to use the famous categories of Machiavelli) have put in a position to control the destiny of a state. The main criteria by which good and bad government have traditionally been distinguished are twofold: government for the common good as opposed to government for personal gain; government according to established laws, whether natural or divine, or based on traditional usage or on sound laws laid down by predecessors but which have become part of the country's established custom, as opposed to arbitrary rule, whose decisions are made *ad hoc* and independently of any pre-established rules. What can be inferred from these two criteria are two distinct but not unrelated images of the type of ruler to be abhorred: the tyrant who abuses power to satisfy illicit personal desires, of whom Plato talks in Book IX of the *Republic*; and the ruler who autonomously creates laws, or the autocrat in the etymological sense of the term.

### RULE UNDER LAWS

The debate over the superiority of the rule of law constantly recurs, without ever being definitively resolved, throughout the history of Western thought (and had an equally important place in ancient China).

One of the most ancient ways of expressing the idea of good government is the Greek term 'eunomia', used by Socrates, the great legislator of Athens, to distinguish it from its opposite 'dysnomia'. The most famous statement concerning the sovereignty of the law for the ancients, and hence repeated countless times by moderns, is contained in a fragment by Pindarus, which has come down to us with the title *Nomos Basiléus*. Without knowing the full context its precise meaning is difficult to establish, but the fragment starts by saying that law is the queen of all things, whether mortal or immortal.[7] Among the seminal passages that the classical era has bequeathed to subsequent ages is Cicero's maxim according to which '*Omnes legum servi sumus uti liberi esse possumus*'. ('We are all slaves of the laws so that we can be free.')[8]

The whole of medieval political thought is dominated by the idea that good rulers are ones who rule in compliance with those laws which they are not free to change at will because they transcend personal volition, being either ordained by God, or written into the nature of things, or established as the foundation of the state's constitution (the 'fundamental' laws). In his *De legibus et consuetudinibus Angliae*, Henri Bracton enunciated a precept destined to become the principle of the juridical state: '*Ipse autem rex non debet esse sub homine sed sub deo et sub lege quia lex facit regem*.'[9] One could not put the idea of the primacy of law more strongly: the king does not make the law, the law makes the king. In the dynamic conception of the legal system developed by modern thinkers ('dynamic' in the sense of the normative theory of Kelsen), Bracton's precept can be translated into the assertion that sovereigns act as legislators only if they exercise power in accordance with the basic norms of the legal system and are thus legitimate sovereigns. They thus only exercise the power to initiate legislation (or establish the norms valid and binding on the whole of society) within the formal and material limits laid down by the constitutional norms, and thus are no tyrants (in the sense of a tyranny '*ex parte exercitii*' as in a military dictatorship).

From England the principle of the 'rule of law' passed into the legal doctrines of continental states giving rise to a doctrine, now universally recognized (in the sense that it is no longer contested by anyone in principle, so much so that when statesmen do not observe it they invoke a state of emergency or exceptional circumstances), of the 'legal state'. In other words the state whose guiding principle is the subordination of power at whatever level, from the humblest to the most exalted, to the principle of law via the process of formally legalizing every act of government. This has come to be known, since the first written constitution of the modern age, as 'constitutionalism'. Two extremely revealing manifestations of the universality of this tendency for political power to be subject to the juridical can be cited. One is the Weberian interpretation of the modern state as a rational legal state, i.e. as a state whose legitimacy resides exclusively in the exercise of power in accordance with laws. The other is the Kelsenian theory of the legal system as a chain of norms which create powers and powers which create norms, the start of which is represented not by the power of powers, as sovereignty has always been conceived in the theory of public law which came into being contemporaneously with the emergence of the modern state, but by the norm of norms, the *Grundnorm*, on which depends the validity of all the norms of the system and the legitimacy of all powers lower down the chain.[10]

## RULE THROUGH LAW

To round off this aspect of the discussion it is necessary to consider the fact that the 'rule of law' can mean two different things, even if they are closely connected: apart from government *sub lege* which is what we have been considering so far, it can also refer to government *per leges*, i.e. via laws, in other words through the widespread, though not necessarily exclusive, promulgation of general, abstract norms. It is one thing for government to exercise power according to pre-established legal principles, it is another for it to exercise power through the intermediary of general legislation rather than specific and concrete decrees. The two expedients are not co-terminous: in a legal or juridical state the judge, when he pronounces a sentence which is a specific and concrete decree, is exercising power *sub lege* but not *per leges*. On the other hand the first legislator, the constituent legislator, exercises power not *sub lege* (unless we postulate, as Kelsen does, a basic norm) but *per leges* at the very moment of drawing up a written constitution. In the formation of the modern state the development of the doctrine of constitutionalism, which subsumes all forms of government *sub lege*, goes hand in hand with the development of the doctrine of the primacy of the legislature as the source of law. The law comes to be understood, on the one hand, as the highest expression of the will of the sovereign, whether the prince or the people, and hence represents a break with rule based on custom, and on the other as a general, abstract norm, and as such opposed to *ad hoc* decrees. If we consider the three greatest philosophers whose theories signal the rise of the modern state, Hobbes, Rousseau and Hegel, it is questionable whether they can be counted among the defenders of the rule of law, but they are all champions of the primacy of the legislature as the source of law, as the main instrument of government and hence the main prerogative of the sovereign power.

This distinction between government *sub lege* and government *per leges* is necessary not only for reasons of conceptual clarity, but also because the virtues that are usually attributed to the rule of law change significantly according to whether it refers to the first or the second. As has been said, the virtues of government *sub lege* consist in preventing, or at least hindering, the abuse of power. the virtues of government *per leges* are different. In fact it could be said that most of the reasons for preferring the rule of law over the rule of men, starting from those adopted by writers in antiquity, have been connected with the exercise of power via general and abstract norms. The various basic principles which the champions of the rule of law have invoked at different times, equality, security and liberty, are all three guaranteed more by the intrinsic character of law when conceived as a general, abstract norm than by the legal exercise of power.

There can be no doubt that the capacity of law to promote equality stems from the nature of the general norm as one which applies not just to an individual but to a class of individuals, and which can even be formed by all the members of a social group. Precisely because of its general frame of reference, a law, whatever it may be, and thus irrespective of its specific provisions, does not admit, at least within the parameters of the category of citizens to whom it applies, either privilege, i.e. provisions to be made to the advantage of a particular individual, or discrimination, or provisions to the disadvantage of a particular individual. The fact that there can exist egalitarian and non-egalitarian laws is another matter: it is a problem that concerns not the form of the law but its contents.

By contrast the capacity of law to provide security depends on another purely formal characteristic of law, namely its abstractness, which enables a given consequence to be linked to the commitment of acts or the carrying out of transactions which are typical and as such predictable and repeatable. In this case the abstract norm contained in the law is distinct from a decree which compels a person or class of persons (in this respect it does matter which) to commit a specific action with a particular end in mind, the performance of which exhausts once and for all the effective force of the decree. While classical theorists, who were keenly aware of the threat posed by tyrannical government, stressed above all the egalitarian function of law, modern writers (I am thinking of Weber's category of the legal rational state) have principally extolled the function government can perform by issuing abstract norms which have the effect of ensuring that the consequences of their own actions are predictable and thus calculable, thereby favouring the development of economic exchange.

The relationship between law and freedom is more problematic. Cicero's famous dictum which states that we must be slaves of the law to be free, if taken at face value, can appear like a rhetorical exhortation to blind obedience. But what is its deeper meaning? There are two possible ways of taking it according to whether we have negative or positive freedom in mind. The interpretation based on positive freedom is the most straightforward, as can be seen in this passage from Rousseau: 'You are always free when you submit to the laws, but not when you submit to a man; for in the second case I must obey the will of someone else, whereas when I obey the laws I am only complying with the public will, which is as much mine as anyone else's.'[11] This interpretation is more straightforward but also more limited in its scope: by 'law' Rousseau means solely the norm promulgated by the general will. Could the same be said of the law decreed by the enlightened legislator, or of a law based on custom or at least of a law not formulated by the general will? Could it be argued that, apart from generality and abstractness, a third intrinsic feature of the law is that it emanates from the general will? If not, is what guarantees the upholding of positive liberty the law in itself or only the law which all have contributed to formulating who will thereafter have to obey it?

To include among the basic attributes of law the safeguard of negative liberty as well requires an even greater limitation of its meaning. It means considering as genuine laws only those norms of conduct which intervene to restrict the behaviour of individuals solely with a view to enabling all of them to enjoy their own private sphere of liberty protected from the interference of others. However strange and historically untenable it may be, this interpretation of the 'authentic' nature of law is anything but uncommon in the history of legal thought. It relates to the theory, possibly pioneered by, but certainly popularized by Thomasius, according to which the distinctive trait of law as opposed to morality consists in its being made up exclusively of negative precepts, which can be summed up in the principle *neminem laedere*. For Hegel too, abstract law, which is the law that jurists deal with, is composed entirely of negatives. This old doctrine which we could call 'the limits of the function of law' (which historically complements the doctrine of the limits of state power) has been salvaged from obscurity and brought to public attention by one of the most important champions of the liberal state, Friedrich von Hayek, who counts as legal norms, in the strict sense of the term, only those which guarantee the conditions or means whereby the individual can freely pursue his or her own ends without being prevented from doing so, except by the equal right of others to do the same thing. It is no coincidence that laws defined in this way represent for Hayek negative imperatives or vetoes.[12]

While the connection between laws and equality is a direct one, for the connection between law and freedom to be justified it is necessary to tamper with the very concept of law by adopting a selective, one-sidedly positive concept of it with overt ideological implications. The proof of this is the fact that to demonstrate the link between the law and positive freedom it is necessary to invoke the democratic doctrine of the state, while the connection between law and negative freedom can only be based on the premisses of liberal doctrine.


### THE RULE OF MEN

Appearing alongside the notion of the primacy of law we find, though admittedly less prominently, parallel arguments for the primacy of the rule of men. However, unlike the first theory, whose history has been traced on many occasions, this latter has never to my knowledge been the specific object of academic research or detailed investigation. Yet it is a phenomenon so vast and varied that it provides ample material for a taxonomic analysis. The following can be considered the tentative first draft of such an exercise.

I start from the premiss that it is essential not to confuse the doctrine of the primacy of the rule of men with the eulogy of monarchy as the ideal form of government, so frequent among such classical political thinkers as Bodin, Hobbes, Montesquieu and Hegel. Monarchical rule, in contrast to tyrannical rule, is always government *sub lege*. Ulpianus's precept, '*princeps legibus solutus est*', which was formulated with Roman heads of state in mind, comes to be interpreted by medieval jurists to mean that the king is not bound by the positive laws he himself decrees or by customs which remain in force only as long as they are tolerated, but is still bound by divine and natural laws to which even a monarch is subject, since over and above being a king he is a man like any other, even if only in his conscience. As St Thomas Aquinas makes clear, for example, what applies in this case is a *vis directiva* rather than a *vis coactiva*.[13] The negative mirror-image of the king is the tyrant, whose power is *extra legem* both in the sense of not having any valid authority to rule, and in the sense of ruling illegally. Even among those writers who regard monarchy as the best form of government, tyranny, the archetypal form of the rule of men, is always portrayed in negative terms. The excellence of monarchy lies, if anything, not in the fact that it is the rule of men as opposed to the rule of law, but, on the contrary, in the fact that monarchs find themselves obliged to respect universally humane laws more than an assembly of nobles or even worse of the people. As long as the rule of men is identified with tyrannical rule there is no reason whatsoever to reverse the ancient doctrine of the primacy of the rule of law. In point of fact the existence in history of tyrannies is, *on the contrary*, an empirical argument for the excellence of the rule of law.

Ever since Plato's famous description of the advent of tyranny due to the dissolution of the *polis* brought about by the 'licentiousness' of democracy (Machiavelli's term), tyranny as a form of government has been much more associated with democracy than with monarchy. However at the beginning of the last century, in the aftermath of the French Revolution and Napoleon's reign as emperor, conservative political writers devoted considerable space to a new category of government, one which from the start has mainly negative connotations. I am referring to so-called 'Caesarism', which with Napoleon III, largely through the influence of Marx's criticism, came to be known also as 'Bonapartism'. Well, all theorists who see in Caesarism an autonomous form of government define it as 'popular tyranny' (or 'despotism') – a clear indication of the continued influence of Platonic ideas, which have been passed down through the centuries along with the hatred of demagogues. In other words Caesarism (or Bonapartism) is the form of rule by one man which comes about as a result of the turmoil and chaos which inevitably follows on the heels of popular government: Jacobinism gives rise to Napoleon the Great, the revolution of 1848 throws up a lesser Napoleon, in just the same way that the ancient tyrant emerged in the Greek cities immediately after the *demos* has gained the upper hand, and the *signore* takes control over the riotous Italian *comuni* in the late Middle Ages. For Tocqueville a new sort of oppression threatens democratic nations to which the classical terms of political analysis do not apply 'because the phenomenon is new'. But not so new that it cannot be described as a form of despotism:

> I seek to trace the novel features under which despotism may appear in the world. The first thing that strikes the observation is an innumerable multitude of men all equal and alike, incessantly endeavouring to procure the petty and paltry pleasures of which they glut their lives ... Above this race of men stands an immense and tutelary power, which takes upon itself alone to secure their gratifications, and to watch over their fate. That power is absolute, minute, regular, provident and mild.[14]

Towards the end of the century considerable space is devoted to the historical and theoretical analysis of Caesarism in two of the most important treatises on politics, those of Treitschke and Roscher. The first, an inveterate Francophobe, argues that Napoleon has satisfied the inner compulsion of the French to be slaves, and calls the regime which emerged from the revolution 'democratic despotism'.[15] The second takes up the classical theme that anarchy provokes the desire for order, one lion always being preferable to ten wolves or a hundred jackals, and expounds the process by which the government of the people produces the tyrant who proceeds to rule with the support of those whom he treats as slaves.[16] As can be seen, the association between popular government and tyranny is a theme beloved of anti-democratic writers, all of whom can trace their ancestry back to Plato. As long ago as the eighteenth century Hamilton was already writing in his critique of Greek democracy in the first *Federalist*: 'of those men who have overturned the liberties of republics, the greatest number have begun their career by paying an obsequious court to the people, commencing demagogues and ending tyrants.'[17]

PATERNALISM

The rule of men as an alternative to the rule of law is portrayed in its most rudimentary form using the image of the sovereign as father or head of a family, i.e. the paternalistic or patriarchal, in extreme cases even despotic, conceptions of power, which occur in those doctrines where the state is conceived as a family writ large, either paternalistic, patriarchal or authoritarian in structure, with a corresponding type of power being wielded by the sovereign. The family, whether large or small, authoritarian or only paternalistic, has always been taken as a model, at least until Locke, of the monocratic system where the highest power is concentrated in the hands of a sole individual and his subjects are in the legal sense of the word 'incompetent', either temporarily, as in the case of children before they came of age, or permanently, as in the case of slaves. Like the father (or patriarch, or head of the household), the king, conceived as the glorified head of a family, is called upon to exercise power not on the basis of pre-established norms and via general and abstract precepts, but in the light of his own wisdom and using *ad hoc* measures adopted in the light of the needs of the moment which only he is authorized to judge. The bonds which link the father or the patriarch to the members of the family household are not legal but ethical, or, at the opposite extreme, founded on sheer force. As a society of unequals – the wife (or wives in the polygamous family) with respect to the husband, the sons with respect to the father, the slaves with respect to the master – the household, and also the state when it is conceived as a family, are not subject to the egalitarian force of the law. Instead their ordering principle is more *ad hoc* justice than legal justice. Equity, or justice applied in a concrete case, can be redefined as the justice of the rule of men instead of that of the rule of law. Even if it is only a side-issue rather than a dominant theme, the ideal of a paternalistic government found in the works of Filmer (and subsequently refuted by Locke) takes us right up to the threshold of the modern age. When Leibniz lists the duties of the sovereign to distinguish good from bad government he is in actual fact repeating the duties associated with the good head of the household. They are duties which concern almost exclusively the proper education and well-being of the subjects, such as inculcating the principles of moderation, prudence, physical health, and the exercise of every physical and spiritual virtue. The latter include the prince's duty to ensure that his subjects' obedience 'is accompanied by admiration and respect' (which echoes the commandment 'Honour your father and mother.')[18] It is no coincidence if the definitive critique of the paternalistic conception of power comes from a thinker like Kant to whom we owe one of the most comprehensive and coherent theories of the juridical state. For Kant, 'a government might be founded on the principle of benevolence towards the people, like that of a father towards his children.' This 'paternal government (*imperium paternale*) ... is the greatest conceivable despotism'.[19]

Ever since the Greeks, and once again it is Aristotle who is the starting point of a tradition destined to last for centuries, the government of the authoritarian sovereign, i.e. despotism, in contrast to tyranny, is a legitimate government, because in a situation where peoples are by nature slaves (and oriental barbarians are considered as such) the only possible form of government is that of the slave-master. In the history of European political thought there are few ideas so tenaciously clung to and monotonously repeated as this one, which is perpetuated by Montesquieu and survives right up to Hegel, who states that in the oriental world 'only one is free', while in the European society of his day, which had started with the Germanic monarchies, 'all are free.'

## THE LEGISLATOR

The archetypal figure associated with the superiority, and to some extent the necessity, of the rule of a wise man rather than of good laws is the great legislator. This figure is indispensible because he overcomes a weakspot in the argument in support of the rule of law, which, it is true, must at some point actually answer the question: 'Where do laws derive from?' The question is so crucial that Plato's *The Laws* opens with these words. The Athenian turns to Clinia and asks him: 'To whom is the merit of instituting your laws ascribed, gentlemen? To a god, or to some man?' And Clinia replies: 'Why to a god, sir, indubitably to a god.'[20]

If we were to reply that laws originate from other laws it would plunge us into an infinite regression. We must stop somewhere. Well then, either the laws have a divine origin or their origin is lost in the dawn of time. But what must be taken into account is that every so often gods inspire outstanding men to establish new laws and so give the cities a lasting and just order: Minos in Crete, Lycurgus at Sparta, Solon at Athens. Seen in this way the relationship between the rule of law and the principle of good government is turned completely on its head: it is not good law which makes the good ruler but the wise legislator who brings about good government by introducing good laws. Men come before laws: the assumption that the rule of law produces good government (and it cannot be if the laws its own actions have to comply with are not good) presupposes the just man who is capable of interpreting the needs of his city. As proof of the considerable suggestive force the idea of the great legislator has exerted over the minds of past generations, it is sufficient to point out that the description *conditor legis* was one of the most glorious titles of which a sovereign could boast.

The ideal of the great legislator was clearly close to the hearts of the Age of Reason, for whom one of the tasks of the enlightened princes seems to be to revive the memory of the emperor Justinian by promoting the work of legislative reform through the drawing up of new legal codes. One of the most surprising and controversial passages in the *Social Contract* is where Rousseau too, admirer of the way Sparta is ruled, pays homage to it: 'Only Gods can give laws to men', he exclaims, echoing the sentiments of the ancient Greeks. After an explicit reference to Plato's concept of the 'Royal' man, he asks: 'But if it be true that a great prince occurs but rarely, what shall be said of the great Law-giver?' The answer is unequivocal: 'The first has but to follow the rules laid down by the latter.' In every respect the legislator must be 'an extraordinary figure', whose self-imposed historic mission is none other than 'to change the very stuff of human nature', 'to transform every individual who, in isolation, is a complete but solitary whole, into a part of something greater than himself.'[21] The myth of the great legislator also inspires governments in the wake of the French Revolution. It is then that the 'science of legislation' flourishes, for which Gaetano Filangeri's monumental work provided an unsurpassed model disseminated among educated circles throughout Europe. The last representative of this tradition before Saint-Simon's critique of 'jurists' left its mark, was

Jeremy Bentham, tireless author of ill-fated legislative projects designed to inaugurate the reign of happiness on earth.

Analogous to the figure of the great legislator is the founder of a state. In this respect the outstanding hero in classical literature, that inexhaustable supply of paradigms in any context, is Theseus, whom Plutarch (who associates him with Romulus, founder of Rome) writes of as someone who 'took a scattered people and made of them a city'. Analogous because it too owes its fascination to the mystery of the origins of things. Every state, if examined both at a given moment of its history and across successive moments, has its own constitution, i.e. a system made up of laws either inherited from the past or newly decreed. But would not someone who wanted to work backwards in time from constitution to constitution not inevitably arrive at the moment when order is born from chaos, the people from the multitude, the city from isolated individuals warring with each other? While the city can be known in its historical development through a study of its laws, its constitutions (or what nowadays we would call its legal system) if we go back to its very beginnings we will not find laws, but men, or rather, if we are to believe the most reliable and widely accepted interpretation, one man, the hero.

It is no accident if the highest tribute to the founder of states, and by this token the most whole-hearted recognition of the primacy of the rule of men over the rule of law, is to be found in a work like *The Prince* by Machiavelli, an author who, as one would expect from the annotator of Livy, had been reared on the humanistic studies and was particularly receptive to the teachings of classical authorities. Speaking of the 'new princes', the most 'excellent' of whom are, according to ancient tradition, Moses, Cyrus, Theseus and Romulus, Machiavelli writes that anyone who considers their works will find all these men 'wondrous'. In the last pages, appealing for the new prince who will have to liberate Italy from its present 'barbarous dominion', he alludes to their example once more and repeats that 'nothing honours a man more than to establish new laws and new ordinances when he himself was newly arisen.'[22] Following in the footsteps of Machiavelli, whom he greatly admires, Hegel places the figure of the hero, the founder of states, at the summit of world history: 'But right is on their side because they are the far-sighted ones: they have discerned what is true in their world and their age . . . and the others flock to their banner.'[23] But have they right on their side? What does this mean? It means, as is made clear in his lectures on the 'Philosophy of Right', that the founders of states have the right, one denied to all their successors, to exercise force over and above existing laws in order to accomplish their extraordinary mission, a right which, since it is not impeded by the rights of others, can justly be called 'absolute'.[24]

## DICTATORSHIP

Both the great legislator, the sage, and the founder of states, the hero, are outstanding individuals who appear in exceptional situations and perform their deeds either in moments of upheaval or at the dawn of a new age. In reality, the rule of men is not so much an alternative to the rule of law as a necessary substitute for it in times of crisis. Nearly all the historical figures who are associated down the ages with the notion of the superiority of the rule of men fit into the category of outstanding individuals. Thus the question 'the rule of men or the rule of law' turns out to be misconceived, because one does not exclude the other. The only situation where the rule of men is portrayed as something positive which is not immediately associated with exceptional circumstances is the one Plato envisages, where the state is presided over by the philosopher-king, but even in Plato's mind he is only an ideal figure. His historical existence is adumbrated in the *Seventh Epistle*, in the phrase 'the human race will not see better days until either the stock of those who rightly and genuinely follow philosophy acquire political power, or else the class who have political control be led by some dispensation of providence to become real philosophers.'[25] But the attempt to institute it ends in failure. Historically the rule of men appears on the scene when the rule of law either has not yet come about or else reveals its inadequacy to cope with the emergence of a revolutionary situation. In short, it is intimately bound up with exceptional circumstances.

Such exceptional circumstances gave rise to the institution of a dictatorship in the first centuries of the Roman republic. It is around this instititution that the most interesting and penetrating reflections on the rule of men have revolved in the past and continue to do so. The Roman dictator is the paradigm for the attribution to a sole person of all powers, of 'full powers', and hence the suspension, even if only temporarily, of the validity of normal laws brought about by a particularly serious threat to the very survival of the state. It neatly illustrates the fact that any assessment of the rule of men must take into account the circumstances which make it necessary. Many of the major political theorists since the Renaissance, from Machiavelli to Rousseau, cite the Roman dictatorhip as an example of political wisdom, in so far as it acknowledges the value of the rule of men but allows it only in the case of public danger and only for the duration of the danger. Indeed, the task of the dictator is precisely that of restoring the state to normality and with it the sovereignty of the law.

Even when dictatorship, violating the principles which constitute it in the first place, tends to prolong itself indefinitely, and an outstanding individual comes on the scene who transforms the constitutional power of the dictator *pro tempore* into personal power, the justification of the indefinite extension of full powers is always based on the exceptional gravity of the crisis which makes it impossible to predict how long it will last. Normally this involves a catastrophic crisis, not a crisis within the regime whose conclusion allows the running of the state to resume its normal course, but an external one which precludes the possibility of moving smoothly from one administration to another. Instead, a world-historical individual appears (to use Hegel's expression), marking the tumultuous transition, as embodied in a long and bloody civil war, from republic to autocracy. The distinction introduced by Carl Schmitt between commissary and sovereign dictatorship reflects the difference between the full powers which exist as an institution provided for by the constitution and the full powers assumed without the sanction of the constitution by a leader who sets out to overthrow the former regime and inaugurate a new one. This difference does not preclude both of them from belonging to the same category of power, that of exceptional or temporary power, even if in the second case the duration of the dictatorship is not constitutionally laid down in advance. Whether the sovereign or constituent dictatorship is then exercised by an individual, like Caesar or Napoleon, or by a political group, like the Jacobins or the Bolsheviks, or even by a whole class, as in the Marxist conception of the state, where it comes to be called the dictatorship of the bourgeoisie or of the proletariat, does not alter the fact that dictatorial rule is one where by definition people repudiate the supremacy of traditional laws. What can change radically are the connotations it can be given: while the commissary dictatorship generally has positive associations, constituent dictatorship can take on positive or negative ones according to which of the various interpretations is applied, so that the Jacobin or Bolshevik dictatorships are praised to the skies by some and bitterly denounced by others. In the language of Marxism, the dictatorship of the bourgeoisie is the reality to be overthrown and that of the proletariat the ideal to be achieved.

Despite the various historical and conceptual distinctions that have to be made between the different forms that power in the hands of one man can take, they all share certain features which are often brought out clearly when the same individual is interpreted as embodying more than one of the forms. It has already been pointed out how anti-democratic writers postulated the existence of a close link between Caesarism and popular dictatorship. But just as frequently invoked, and with equal historical justification, is the link between Caesarism and dictatorship. Franz Neumann, for example, talks of a 'Caesaristic dictatorship' as one of three types of dictatorship (the others being simple and totalitarian dictatorship), and quotes the (unusual) example of the ephemeral rule of Cola di Rienzo, defining it as 'one of the most fascinating of Caesaristic dictatorships'.[26] Associating Caesarism with tyranny throws into relief above all those features of it which epitomize the corruption of power. To associate it with dictatorship highlights the way it exists as an exceptional form of government, which, being justified by a state of emergency, is not negative *per se*. These two aspects are not mutually exclusive, even if tyrannical power is not always exceptional and exceptional power is not always corrupt. According to the Marxist interpretation of the *coup d'état* of Louis Bonaparte, 'Bonapartism' more closely resembles dictatorship than tyranny. That is to say it represents the exercise of exceptional powers in a situation where the power of the ruling class is under threat (the situation, incidentally, which had been anticipated in the Roman institution of dictatorship, since it could be invoked not only in the case of external dangers but also internal ones). Following Marx, Gramsci defines Caesarism as characteristic of a 'situation in which the forces in conflict balance each other in a catastrophic manner; that is to say they balance each other in such a way that a continuation of the conflict can only terminate in their reciprocal destruction'.[27] Furthermore Gramsci distinguishes a progressive Caesarism from a regressive one, pointing to Caesar and Napoleon I as examples of the first type, and Bismarck and Napoleon III as examples of the second. These pages of the *The Prison Notebooks* were written between 1932 and 1934: it is not stretching the imagination too much to guess that when talking of progressive Caesarism he had Lenin in mind, and that regressive Caesarism corresponded for him to Mussolini.

### CHARISMATIC AND LEGAL-RATIONAL RULE

We have to wait until Max Weber to have the first comprehensive theory of power which is both personal and exceptional. One of Weber's three categories of legitimate power is the famous one of charismatic power. To round off this rapid survey of the subject, it would not be too simplistic to say that Weber's charismatic leader is a sort of synthesis of all the forms of the rule of men that can be discerned in history. It brings together traits of the great demagogue (the tyrant of classical times, who provides material for the modern form of Caesarism), the hero in the Machiavellian and Hegelian senses, and the great military leader. It does not, however, include the great legislators, who receive marginal treatment by Weber, who only has to say of them that they 'were generally, though not always, called to their office when social tensions were in evidence to resolve the conflicts between status groups and to produce a new sacred law of eternal validity.'[28]

At the opposite pole from charismatic power stands legal power: taken together the two are the perfect symbols of the dichotomy between the rule of men and the rule of law. Traditional power lies somewhere between the two extremes; it is a form of personal power but not extraordinary: it is a personal power whose legitimacy derives not from the qualities of the leader but from the force of tradition and hence, as in the case of legal power, from an impersonal force. Charismatic power, in contrast to the other two, is the product of the great crises of the past, whereas legal and traditional power represent the long intervening periods of relative calm in between. Charismatic power flares up in those brief and intense periods which come between an end and a beginning, between decadence and regeneration, between the death agony of the old order and the birth pangs of the new. If its ascendancy is usually ephemeral, its task is nonetheless extraordinary.

It is futile to ask Weber which is better, the rule of men or the rule of law: he is famous for his declaration that the task of the academic is not to give value judgements but to understand (*verstehen*), and that a university chair is neither for prophets nor for demagogues (two incarnations of charismatic power). Considered objectively, the rule of a charismatic leader, like that of law, is neither good nor bad. Nor are they arbitrarily interchangeable. They are diferent manifestations of distinct historical circumstances, which the social scientist must do justice to by accumulating as much historical and empirical data as possible (and in this respect Weber is unsurpassed), so as to elaborate a theory of the forms power can take which is as comprehensive as possible, exhaustive and *wertfrei*. The fact that Weber, as a committed political writer, should have had his own preferences, and in the last years of his life developed the ideal of a form of mixed government which combined the legitimacy of a democracy with the active presence of a leader which he called 'plebiscitary democracy' to distinguish it from a leaderless or 'headless' democracy, is a problem that we do not need to go into in this context. Especially since the plebiscitary democracy that actually came about in Germany a few years after his death was certainly not the one which he had envisaged and so warmly championed. In any case, nothing can take away from Weber the achievement of having, better than any other theorist, found the right terms in which to formulate one of the oldest problems in political philosophy, translating a debate between the protagonists of diametrically opposed points of view, into a complex theoretical model, the choice between the alternatives being a matter for the politician and not the scientist.

If, then, at the end of this analysis, I am asked to take off the mortar-board of the academic and put on the hat of someone deeply involved in the political developments of the age he lives in, I have no hesitation in saying that my preference is for the rule of law rather than of men. The rule of law is now celebrating its final triumph as the basis of the democratic system. What is democracy other than a set of rules (the so- called rules of the game) for the solution of conflicts without bloodshed? And what constitutes good democratic government if not rigorous respect for these rules? I for one have no doubts about how such questions are to be answered. And precisely because I have no doubts I can conclude in all good conscience that democracy is the rule of law *par excellence*. The very moment a democracy loses sight of this, its inspiring principle, it rapidly reverts into its opposite, into one of the many forms of autocratic government which haunt the chronicles of historians and the speculations of political thinkers.

# Notes

INTRODUCTION

1 See G. Duncan and S. Lukes, 'The New Democracy', *Political Studies*, XI, (1963), pp. 156–77 for an influential analysis of the competing claims of 'empirical' and 'normative' theories of democracy written from a radical perspective largely critical of the former. For a powerful critique of both schools of thought, stressing how both sides have hijacked the positive connotations accociated with any political system calling itself democratic, see Q. Skinner, 'The Empirical Theorists of Democracy and their Critics: A plague on both their houses', *Political Theory*, I (1973), pp. 287–306.

2 For a discussion of Turin university life at this time see Gioele Solari 'Aldo Mautino nella tradizione culturale torinese da Gobetti alla resistenza' in A. Mautino, *La formazione della filosofia politica di Benedetto Croce*, (Laterza, Bari, 1953), pp. 3–132. The influence of Crocean idealism on Italian cultural life is traced in R. Bellamy, 'Liberalism and Historicism: Benedetto Croce and the political role of idealism in modern Italy *c.* 1890–1952'. A. Moulakis, (ed.) *The Promise of History* (W. de Gruyter, Berlin/New York, 1986), pp. 69–119. The whole period is splendidly described by Bobbio in his *Profilo ideologico del novecento italiano*, (Einaudi: Turin, 1986).

3 For a discussion of the two schools of thought in Turin at the time, albeit with a bias towards the Gramscian faction, see A. Asor Rosa, 'Torino operaia e capitalista', in *Storia d'Italia* IV ii, (Einaudi, Turin 1975), pp. 1439–64. Norberto Bobbio gives a sympathetic account of reformist socialism in his *Profilo*, pp. 62–73.

4 Carlo Rosselli, *Socialismo liberale*, [1929]. (Einaudi, Turin, 1973), p. 451.

5 Ibid., p. 454.

6 Ibid., p. 445.

7 On Carlo Rosselli see A. Garosci, *La vita di Carlo Rosselli*, (2 vols, Edizioni U, Rome/Florence/Milan, 1946), and N. Tranfaglia, *Carlo Rosselli dall' interventismo a 'Giustizia e Libertà'*, (Laterza, Bari, 1968).

8 N. Bobbio, *Saggi sulla scienze politica in Italia*, (Laterza, Bari, 1971), pp. 247–8 and Ch. IX.

158     NOTES TO INTRODUCTION

9  Most of these studies are collected in his *Saggi sulla scienza politica*.
10 Guido de Ruggiero's *History of European Liberalism* (1924) tr. R. G. Collingwood, (Oxford University Press, Oxford, 1927) is an eloquent example of this Italian literature. Fuller details of this movement are given in R. Bellamy 'An Italian "new liberal" theorist: Guido de Ruggiero's *History of European Liberalism*', *Historical Journal*, forthcoming. Hobhouse, Hobson and G. D. H. Cole were the most influential English thinkers.
11 See '*Il Movimento Operaio*' (1924) and '*Battaglia Storica*' (1926) in C. Rosselli, *Socialismo Liberale*, pp. 65–77, 77–79.
12 Donald Sassoon *The Strategy of the Communist Party from the Resistance to the Historic Compromise*, (Frances Pinter, London, 1981), and Anne Showstack Sassoon, *Gramsci's Politics*, (Croom Helm, London, 1980), are influential sophisticated accounts in the hagiographical tradition. For a useful corrective see T. Judt, '"The Spreading Notion of the Town": Some Recent Writings on French and Italian Communism', *Historical Journal*, XXVIII, (1985), pp. 1011–21.
13 N. Bobbio, *Quale Socialismo?: Discussione di un'alternativa*, (Einaudi, Turin, 1976). The terms of this debate can also be traced to an earlier discussion between the 'Giustizia e Libertà' group and the PCI. See G. Amendola's 'Con il proletariato o contro il proletariato?', *Lo Stato Operaio* V, June 1931, p. 6 and the 'Risposta a Giorgio Amendola', in *Quaderni di giustizia e libertà*, I, Jan. 1932, p. 40. The discussion was continued after the war in the famous exchange between Bobbio and Galvano della Volpe in the 1950s. Details of these disputes are given in R. Bellamy, *Modern Italian Social Theory*, (Polity Press, Cambridge, 1987), ch. 7.
14 Marx's most trenchant criticisms of 'bourgeois *Recht*' occur in 'On the Jewish Question', in *Early Writings*, tr. R. Livingstone and G. Benton, (Penguin, Harmondsworth, 1975), pp. 211–41. His advocacy of workers' councils can be found in 'The Civil War in France' in David Fernbach (ed.) *The First International and After*, (Penguin, Harmondsworth, 1974), pp. 187–236. Lenin's ideas on the revolutionary party and his attack on social democracy occur in *What is to be Done?*, tr. S. V. and Patricia Utechin, (Oxford University Press, Oxford, 1963). For a concise introduction to their views and failings see M. Levin, 'Marxism and Democratic Theory', in G. Duncan (ed.), *Democratic Theory and Practice*, (Cambridge University Press, Cambridge, 1983), pp. 79–95.
15 p. 26.
16 p. 24.
17 J. A. Schumpeter, *Capitalism, Socialism and Democracy*, (George Allen and Unwin, London, 1943).
18 R. A. Dahl, *Preface to Democratic Theory*, (University of Chicago Press, Chicago, 1956).
19 G. Sartori, *Democratic Theory*, (Wayne State University Press, Detroit, 1962).

20  E.g. Schumpeter, *Capitalism, Socialism, Democracy*, p. 269.
21  E.g. Dahl, *Preface to Democratic Theory*, pp. 133–4.
22  For a discussion of Mosca and modern pluralism see R. Bellamy, *Modern Italian Social Theory*, ch. 3.
23  For an analysis of the underside of Italian politics see P. A. Alum, *Italy– Republic without Government?*, (Weidenfeld and Nicholson, London, 1973), chs. 3 and 4; and Martin Clark, *Italy 1871–1982*, (Longman, London, 1984), pp. 334–8.
24  Dahl, *Preface to Democratic Theory*, p. 137.
25  Ibid., pp. 75–7.
26  Ibid., p. 134.
27  These arguments are elaborated by Jack Lively, *Democracy*, (Basil Blackwell, Oxford, 1975), pp. 21–4.
28  For a critique of American pluralists' blindness to these factors see Steven Lukes, *Power: A Radical View*, (Macmillan, London, 1974).
29  Judith Chubb, *Patronage, Power and Poverty in Southern Italy*, (Cambridge University Press, Cambridge, 1982), provides a chilling account of this side of Italian politics.
30  E.g. G. D. H. Cole, *Self-Government in Industry*, (G. Bell and Sons, London, 1919).
31  E.g. H. Laski, *Studies in the Problem of Sovereignty*, (George Allen and Unwin, London, 1917).
32  Carole Pateman, *Participation and Democratic Theory*, (Cambridge University Press, Cambridge, 1970).
33  Peter Bachrach, *The Theory of Democratic Elitism: a Critique*, (Little, Brown and Co., Boston, 1967).
34  E.g. Showstack Sassoon, *Gramsci's Politics*, p. 227. For an alternative reading see R. Bellamy *Modern Italian Social Theory*, ch. 7.
35  Robert E. Lane, 'From Political to Industrial Democracy?', *Polity*, XVII, (1985), pp. 623–48, provides empirical evidence to support this contention.
36  R. A. Dahl, *After the Revolution?*, (Yale University Press, New Haven and London, 1970), for all its criticisms of participatory democracy, praises workers' self-management on the Yugoslav model pp. 130–40. He has recently developed this argument in *A Preface to Economic Democracy*, (Polity Press, Cambridge, 1985).
37  See F. M. Barnard and R. A. Vernon, 'Pluralism, Participation and Politics: Reflections on the Intermediate Group', *Political Theory*, III, (1975), pp. 180–197; and *Idem* 'Socialist Pluralism and Pluralist Socialism', *Political Studies*, XXV, (1977), pp. 474–90, for useful criticisms along these lines.
38  These ambiguities have been traced by David Miller, 'Democracy and Social Justice', in P. Birnbaum, J. Lively and G. Parry (eds), *Democracy, Consensus and Social Contract*, (Sage, London and Beverley Hills, 1978), pp. 75–100.
39  J. S. Mill, *Utilitarianism, Liberty, Representative Government*, (Dent, London, 1964), p. 283.

40  J.-J. Rousseau, *The Social Contract and Discourses*, (Dent, London, 1968), p. 42.
41  S. Brittan, *The Economic Consequences of Democracy*, (Temple Smith, London, 1977).
42  R. Nozick, *Anarchy, State and Utopia*, (Basic Books: New York, 1975), p. 25.
43  J. Gray, *Liberalism*, (Open University Press: Milton Keynes, 1986), pp. 76–7.
44  p. 116.
45  Ibid.
46  p. 117.
47  J. Rawls, *A Theory of Justice*, (Clarendon Press: Oxford, 1974).
48  J. Rawls, 'Justice as Fairness: Political not Metaphysical', *Philosophy and Public Affairs*, XIV, (1985), pp. 223–51.
49  Ibid., pp. 225–6.
50  Ibid., p. 232.
51  Ibid., p. 220.
52  Ibid., pp. 234–6.
53  Ibid., p. 237.
54  Ibid., p. 231, n. 14.
55  Ibid., p. 245.
56  E.g. V. Haskar, *Equality, Freedom and Perfectionism*, (Clarendon Press, Oxford, 1979), ch. 10.
57  J. Rawls, 'Kantian Constructivism in Moral Theory'. *Journal of Philosophy*, 77, (1980) pp. 526 f.
58  Rawls, 'Justice as Fairness', pp. 248–51.
59  Those interested may consult N. Daniels *Reading Rawls*, (Blackwell, Oxford, 1975), for an overview of some of the early criticisms.
60  In *A Theory of Justice*, pp. 544–5 Rawls explicitly rejected the idea that raising income might be necessary for self-respect. However when, in a recent discussion of his ideas in Oxford, it was pointed out that the 'difference principle' (2ii) entailed regarding democracy as not just a legitimizing device, but as linked to a definite system of income distribution in society, he accepted this. Bobbio certainly believes, rightly or wrongly, that Rawls's theory leads to a form of liberal socialism. See N. Bobbio, G. Pontara, S. Veca, *Crisi della democrazia e neocontrattualismo*, (Riuniti, Rome, 1984), pp. 55–85. R. Plant, *The Market, Equality and the State*, (Fabian Society, London, 1984), similarly notes the bearing of Rawlsian arguments for socialists.
61  p. 32.

CHAPTER 1    THE FUTURE OF DEMOCRACY

1  G. W. F. Hegel, *Lectures on the Philosophy of World History*. tr. H. B. Nibet (Cambridge University Press, Cambridge, 1975), p. 171.
2  H. H. Gerth and C. Wright Mills, (eds), *From Max Weber*, (Routledge and Kegan Paul, London, 1970), p. 146.

3 On this point cf. N. Bobbio, 'Decisioni individuali e collettive', in *Ricerche politiche due (Identità, interessi e scelte collettive)*, (Il Saggiatore, Milan, 1983), pp. 9–30.

4 I have given more extensive consideration to this subject in my chapter 'La regola della maggioranza: limiti e aporie', in N. Bobbio *et al.*, *Democrazia, maggioranza e minoranza*, (Il Mulino, Bologna, 1981), pp. 33–72; and in 'La regola di maggioranza e i suoi limiti' in V. Dini (ed.), *Soggetti e potere. Un dibattito su società civile e crisi della politica*, (Bibliopolis, Naples, 1983), pp. 11–23.

5 V. Pareto, *Trasformazione della democrazia*, (Corbaccio, Milan, 1920), a collection of articles first published in the *Rivista di Milano* between May and July 1920.

6 Johannes Agnoli and Peter Brückner, *Die Transformation der Demokratie*, (Europäische Verlagsanstalt, Frankfurt am Main, 1968).

7 Boris L. Pasternak, *Doctor Zhivago*, tr. M. Hayward and M. Harari (Collins and Harvill Press, London, 1958), p. 460. (The English translation has for the phrase Bobbio quotes 'A thing which has been conceived in a lofty, ideal manner becomes coarse and material'. In this instance the Italian version has been adhered to so that Bobbio's point is not unnecessarily obscured. [Tr.])

8 C. B. Macpherson, *The Political Theory of Possessive Individualism*, (Clarendon Press, Oxford, 1973).

9 For a detailed discussion of this point cf. P. Violante, *Lo spazio della rappresentanza*, (Mozzone, Palermo, 1981), vol. I: Francia 1788–1789.

10 I am referring in particular to the increasingly heated debate which has been provoked in the last few years by the thesis of P. C. Schmitter. For its Italian ramifications cf. M. Maraffi (ed.), *La società neocorporativa*, (Il Mulino, Bologna, 1981), and L. Bordogna and G. Provasi, *Politica, economia e rappresentanza degli interessi*, (Il Mulino, Bologna, 1984).

11 Gaetano Mosca (1858–1941) was a Sicilian political sociologist, whose most famous work, the *Elementi di scienza politica* (1896–1923) was translated into English as *The Ruling Class*. He argued that no matter what political system you adopted, be it autocracy or democracy, power was always held by an oligarchy, or 'political class' possessing the talent appropriate to the social and economic conditions of the age. While he initially criticized democracy as a false and pernicious doctrine, he later sought to adapt it to his elitist model and opposed Fascism. Vilfredo Pareto (1848–1923), in contrast, provides in his *Trattato di sociologia generale* (1916), translated into English as *The Mind in Society*, a justification and handbook for elite rule through the application of force and the use of propaganda. Not surprisingly he became a confirmed antidemocrat and a supporter of Mussolini. See R. Bellamy, *Modern Italian Social theory*, (Polity Press, Cambridge, 1986), chs 2 and 3 for further details. [Ed.]

12 I am referring to R. Dahrendorf, 'Citizenship and Beyond: The Social Dynamics of an Idea', *Social Research*, vol. 41, (1974), pp. 673–701.

(The Italian translation of this article, *Cittadini e partecipazione: al di là della democrazia rappresentativa?*, renders Dahrendorf's key phrase 'the complete citizen' as 'the total citizen', a term also used for the title of the collection of essays in which it appears: *Il cittadino totale*, (Centro di ricerca e documentazione Luigi Einaudi, Turin, 1977). To avoid disturbing the rhetorical effect of Bobbio's argument in this passage, and in the later one on the same concept in ch. 2, I have translated the Italian expression directly. [Tr.])

13  C. B. Macpherson, *The Life and Times of Liberal Democracy*, (Oxford University Press, Oxford, 1977).

14  Cf. F. Burzio, *Essenza e attualità del liberalismo*, (Utet, Turin, 1945), p. 19.

15  Cf. N. Bobbio, 'La democrazia e il potere invisibile', *Rivista italiana di scienza politica*, X (1980), pp. 181–203, reprinted in this volume as ch. 4.

16  A. Wolfe, *The Limits of Legitimacy. Political Contradictions of Contemporary Capitalism*, (The Free Press, New York, 1977).

17  M. Joly, *Dialogue aux enfers entre Machiavel et Montesquieu ou la politique de Machiavel au XIXᵉ siècle par un contemporain*, ('chez tous les libraires', Brussels, 1868).

18  I. Kant, 'Perpetual Peace. A Philosophical Essay', in *Kant's Political Writings*, tr. H. B. Nisbet (Cambridge University Press, Cambridge 1970), p. 126.

19  *The Republic of Plato*, tr. F. M. Camford, (Oxford University Press, Oxford, 1941) ix 571cd, p. 296–7.

20  J. S. Mill, 'Considerations on Representative Government' in *Collected Papers of John Stuart Mill*, (Toronto, University of Toronto Press, Routledge and Kegan Paul, London, 1977) vol. XIX, p. 406.

21  Ibid., p. 470.

22  A. de Tocqueville, '*Discorso sulla rivoluzione sociale*', in *Scritti politici*, ed. N. Matteuci, (Utet, Turin, 1969), vol. I, p. 271.

23  E. Halévy, *L'ère des tyrannies. Études sur le socialisme et la guerre*, preface by C. Bouglé, (Nrf, Paris, 1938).

24  Juan Linz (ed.), *The Breakdown of Democracy*, (The John Hopkins University Press, London, 1978). Its theme is the advent of Fascism in Italy, Germany and Spain.

25  Published by the *Centro de investigaciones sociológicas*, Madrid, 1981.

26  This thesis has been defended recently using theoretical and historical arguments by M. W. Doyle, 'Kant, Liberal Legacies and Foreign Affairs', *Philosophy and Public Affairs*, XII, (1983), pp. 205–35, 323–53.

27  Kant, 'Perpetual Peace', p. 99.

28  K. Popper, *The Open Society and its Enemies*, (Routledge and Kegan Paul, London, 1962), p. 124.

29  Hegel, *Lectures*, cf. p. 69.

CHAPTER 2   REPRESENTATIVES AND DIRECT DEMOCRACY

1  J.-J. Rousseau, 'The Social Contract', in E. Baker (ed.), *Social Contract*, (Oxford University Press, London, 1960), book III 15, p. 262

2  Ibid., book III 4, pp. 232–3.

3  Ibid., p. 232.

4  R. Dahrendorf, 'Citizenship and Beyond: The Social Dynamics of an Idea' in *Social Research*, vol. 41, (1974), pp. 697: 'Societies as a whole become ungovernable if their sectors refuse, in the name of citizenship rights, to be governed, and this in turn cannot fail to affect the ability of sectors to survive: the paradox of The Complete Citizen'. (Cf. ch. 1, footnote 11. [Tr.])

5  Bobbio is referring to the debate aroused by his articles on the nature of socialism, written between 1973–76. Polity Press will be publishing them under the title *What is Socialism?* A review of the debate can be found in R. Bellamy, *Modern Italian Social Theory* (Polity Press, Cambridge, 1987), ch. 8. [Ed.]

6  For a useful introduction to this question cf. M. Cotta 'Rappresentanza politica', in N. Bobbio *et al.* (eds) *Dizionario di politica*, (Utet, Turin, 1983), pp. 954–9 and the various authors cited there.

7  K. Marx, 'The Civil War in France', in *Marx and Engels. Basic Writings on Politics and Philosophy*, ed. L. S. Freuer, (Fontana, London, 1969), p. 401.

8  V. I. Lenin, *State and Revolution* (Library of marxist-Leninist classics, Moscow, 2nd ed., 1951).

9  The Chamber of Fasces and Corporations totally replaced the old parliamentary system in 1939, although its origins go back to the Fascist constitutional reform of 1926 and the National Council of Corporations which dates from 1930. Rather more imposing in name than in fact, it was supposed to replace the old parties and unions by representing people according to their social class and economic function. In this respect it echoed Hegel's theory of the *Stände* and *Korporation* in the *Philosophy of Right*, and its progenitors, Rocco and Gentile, were both Hegelian thinkers. It did not mirror the spirit of his ideas, however, and was hardly more than a bureaucratic creation with little or no foundation in reality. [Ed.]

10  L. Einaudi, 'Rappresentanza di interessi e Parlamento' in *Cronache economiche e politiche di un trentennio*, vol. V, (Einaudi, Turin, 1961), p. 528. (Francesco Ruffini (1863–1934), was a canon lawyer, writer and liberal senator. He spoke out against Fascism from the first, ultimately losing his university post when, with only ten other professors, he refused to swear an oath of loyalty to Fascism. Luigi Einaudi (1874–1961) was a leading liberal economist and a dedicated supporter of deregulation. He was the first president of the Italian Republic, from 1948 to 1955. [Ed.])

11  G. Glotz, *La città greca*, (Einaudi, Turin, 1948).

12  Especially in the United States arguments have been put forward along these lines. cf. Z. Brzezinski, *Between Two Ages: America's Role in the Technocratic Age*, (Viking Press, New York, 1970); and E. G. Tullock, *Private Wants in Public Means: an Economic Analysis of the Desirable Scope of Government*, (Basic Books, New York, 1971).
13  Thucydides, *The Peloponnesian Wars*, tr. R. Warner, (Penguin, London, 1954), p. 118.
14  Rousseau, 'The Social Contract', in *Social Contract*, book III 15, p. 259.
15  A collection of some of the most important articles to appear on pluralism in the Italian press in 1976 were published in *Il pluralismo*, ed. G. Rossini, with a preface by G. Bodrato, (Edizioni Cinque Lune, Rome, 1977).

CHAPTER 3    THE CONSTRAINTS OF DEMOCRACY

1  I have in mind particularly what I said in N. Bobbio, *Quale socialismo?*, (Einaudi, Turin, 1976), pp. 41–45.
2  N. Bobbio *et al.*, *Discutere lo stato*, (De Donato, Bari, 1978).
3  Ibid., 'Il marxismo come teoria infinita ', p. 16.
4  Ibid., 'Teoria dello stato o teoria del partito?', p. 103.
5  A. Asor Rosa, '*La felicità e la politica*', Laboratorio politico, n. 2, (1981), p. 31.
6  The rhyming Italian proverb which Bobbio uses as a metaphor here ('o mangi la minestra o salti questa finestra') translates literally as 'If you do not like the soup then jump out of this window', roughly equivalent to the English 'Take it or leave it' or 'Like it or lump it!'. [Tr.]
7  For more on the theme of the constitutional rules in a democratic system cf. N. Bobbio, 'Norma' in *Enciclopedia Einaudi*, (Einaudi, Turin, 1980), vol. IX, pp. 896–7.
8  Although in existence since 1955, as a left-wing splinter group from the Liberal party, the Radical Party only came to prominence in 1976 when it won four seats in the Italian Chamber. Under its charismatic leader, Marco Pannella, the party managed to treble its vote to 1,250,000 in 1979. Succinctly described as a 'post-materialist' party, the radicals have devoted themselves to a host of issues ignored by the major parties, from divorce and abortion to nuclear power and hunting. They have attempted to gain support for and implement these policies through the holding of referendums, in 1981 gaining the requisite 5 million signatures (500,000 each) for ten separate referendums. The constitutional court only allowed four of them to go to the electorate, a fact which led to a great deal of controversy since two of those disallowed – anti-hunting and the curtailment of the nuclear power programme – had widespread popular support but were opposed by all the other parties. Their disparagement of electoral politics and the rise of the socialists as a leftist alternative to the *Partito Comunista Italiano* has led to a fall in

their vote just recently, but they still have the allegiance of much of the intelligentsia and of influential journals such as *L'Espresso* and *La Repubblica*. [Ed.]

9  The *Legge Truffa*, or 'swindle law' as the Communist Party called it, was an attempt to throw out the proportional principle from the Chamber of Deputies. The ruling coalition of Christian Democrats, Social Democrats, Republicans and Liberals, fearing heavy losses in the 1953 election, enacted legislation whereby the party or coalition receiving over 50 per cent of the votes cast automatically obtained a two-thirds majority in the Chamber. It proved a good rallying point for the opposition and they fell short of the necessary majority by a few hundred votes. The law was repealed the following year. [Ed.]

10  Italian government is mainly by coalition, oscillating between Centrist governments consisting of Christian Democrats, Republicans, Social Democrats and the Liberals and Centre-Left coalitions, excluding the Liberals and including the Socialists. The latter sort prevailed from 1963–1972 and is currently in power. [Ed.]

11  Between 1973–1979 the Communist Party tacitly supported a number of the Christian Democrat policies, a strategy dubbed by their leader, Berlinguer, a 'historical compromise'. This policy was rewarded by a dramatic increase in its share of the vote, the number of Communist deputies rising from 179 in 1972 to 227 in 1976. However, it ultimately alienated some of its traditional supporters, and at the 1979 election its percentage of the vote fell for the first time since 1947, from 34.4 per cent to 30.4 per cent. [Ed.]

12  *The Movimento Sociale Italiano (Destra Nazionale)*, i.e. the Italian Social Movement (National Right), is a neo-fascist organization. It has a relatively constant support, especially in the South, of around 6 per cent of the vote. [Ed.]

13  The period 1968–79 was undoubtedly one of social change in Italy, with reforms such as divorce and abortion being gained in 1974 and 1978 respectively. However, it was equally a period of civil unrest and disappointed expectations, seeing the growth of both left- and right-wing terrorism. [Ed.]

14  A bomb in Piazza Fontana, Milan, in December 1969, killed 14 people and wounded 90 others. Generally attributed to right-wing terrorist groups, members of the government secret services were implicated in the outrage. Although various trials have been held, none has successfully obtained any convictions. [Ed.]

15  *Riflusso*, literally 'ebb', is the Italian term for the political quietism that has ensued in many countries after the high point of political agitation among students and trade unions passed in the early 1970s. Cf. the current German expression *neue Innerlichkeit* [Tr.]

16  F.Erbani, 'Le ambiguità del "Riflusso"', *Nord e Sud*, XXVIII, (1981), pp. 23–33.

17  B. Spinoza, *Letters*, XXX, in The Correspondence of Spinoza, tr. A. Wolf, (G. Allen and Unwin, London, 1928), p. 203

18  This distinction is made by P. Santi in P. Santi *et al.*, *Non tutto è politica*, (Spirali edizioni, Milan, 1981), p. 91.

19  J.-J. Rousseau, '*The Social Contract*' in E. Baker (ed.), Social Contract, (Oxford University Press, London, 1960).

20  V. Pareto (1848–1923) was an Italian economist and sociologist, who spent the latter part of his life in Switzerland as a Professor at Lausanne. He believed human beings are motivated by certain constant psychological dispositions, or 'residues', of which ideas are merely 'derivations'. The social scientist's task is therefore to elaborate the constant features, (Pareto identified 52), from which human behaviour stems. For more detail see Richard Bellamy, *Modern Italian Social Theory*, (Polity Press, Cambridge, 1987), ch. 2. [Ed.]

21  The expression *qualunquismo* dates back to the 1946 elections to the Constituent Assembly, when a new party of the 'average man' or '*uomo qualunque*', won 30 seats. The phrase came to designate the conservatism of the petit-bourgeoisie. [Ed.]

22  This chapter originated as an article prompted by a questionnaire conceived by Luigi Manconi concerning the New Left, the traditional parties in general and the birth of social movements whose policy in practice centre on calls for the right of civil disobedience, of self-determination and veto.

23  I have written at some length on this subject in N. Bobbio, 'La regola di maggioranza: limiti e aporie', in N. Bobbio, C. Offre and S. Lombardini, *Democrazia, maggioranza e minoranze*, (Il Mulino, Bologna, 1981), pp. 33–72.

24  For some further reflections on civil disobedience on the right of veto cf. N. Bobbio 'La resistenza all'oppressione, oggi' in *Studi sassaresi*, (1973) pp. 15–31; and under the entry 'Disobbedienza civile' in *Dizionario di politica*, (Utet, Turin, 1983), pp. 338–42.

25  Jacques de Chabannes, Sieur de la Palisse (*c.* 1470–1525) was a Marshal of France, who died at the battle of Pavia. He was immortalized in song by his soldiers, on account of which he became a byword for obvious truths or platitudes due to the naïvity of the two lines: '*Un quart d'heure avant sa mort, il était encore en vie*'. However, Bobbio may here be alluding not only to the truism contained within his observation but to the Fascist philosopher, Giovanni Gentile (1875–1944) who used the name as a pseudonym in 1937 when attacking changes to his 1922 Education Reform Bill and who held that government is built on force rather than consent. See Bellamy, *Modern Italian Social Theory*, ch. 6. [Ed.]

CHAPTER 4    DEMOCRACY AND INVISIBLE POWER

1  N. Bobbio, *Quale socialismo?*, (Einaudi, Turin, 1976), pp. 45 *et seq.*

2  E.g. in R. Ruletti, 'Il lento cammino verso la verità' in *L'umanità*, (13 Mar. 1980), p. 1.

3  G. Glotz, *La città greca*, (Einaudi, Turin, 1948), p. 202.

4   Plato, *The Laws*, 701a, tr. A. E. Taylor, (Dent and Sons, London, 1960), p. 84. Cf. also an earlier passage in which it is said that music cannot be judged by just anyone, since the judge of good music must not 'learn his verdict from the audience, letting himself be intimidated by the clamour of the multitude and his own incompetence, and form his judgements by taking lessons from spectators.' There follows a criticism of 'the custom of Sicily and Italy, which leaves things to the majority of the audience and decides their victory by their votes'. (659*b*).

5   Nietzsche's use of the term 'theatrocracy' in a passage of *The Wagner Case* is clearly derived from Plato, even if he lays emphasis on the idea of theatre as a place rather than an assembly of spectators. In it he reproaches the Bayreuth movement for having encouraged 'the presumption of the layman, of the art-idiot', which leads to 'these people organising associations, wanting to impose their own taste, and to make themselves judges in rebus musicis et musicantibus', (this phrase certainly derives from Plato). He then claims they have brought about a 'theatrocracy', defined as 'the fantastic notion of the *primacy* of the theatre over the arts, over art'. F. Nietzsche *Werke*, (Walter de Gruyter, Berlin, 1969), VI, 3, p. 36.

6   M. Natale, *Catechismo reppublicano per l'istruzione del popolo e la rovina de'tiranni*, in the recent edition of G. Acocella, (Vico Equense, 1978), p. 71. Another curious remark can be quoted from M. Joly, *Dialogue aux enfers entre Machiavel et Montesquieu ou la politique de Machiavel au XIX^e siècle par un contemporain*, ('chez tous les libraires', Brussels, 1868), p. 25: 'but as publicity is the essence of free countries, all these instititutions could not survive long if they did not function in the clear light of day.'

7   The temporary nature of an exceptional measure is one of the defining features of the type of Roman dictatorship which C. Schmitt defines as 'commissary' to distinguish it from 'sovereign' dictatorship. cf. *Die Diktatur*, (Duncker and Humboldt, Munich, 1921), ch. 1. The exceptional concentration of power is justified by its short duration. From the moment dictatorship becomes permanent the dictator is transformed into a tyrant. Roman dictatorship is a typical example of the justification of the exception to the rule through the limitation of the the period of time for which it is to be violated. Typical in the sense that any exceptional measure, as long as it is rigorously limited in duration, suspends the application of the rule but does not abrogate the rule itself, thus safeguarding the system as a whole.

8   In particular cf. letter n. 10 of 23 November 1787, Max Beloff (ed.), *The Federalist*, (Basil Blackwell, Oxford, 1948), p. 41 *et seq*.

9   C. Schmitt, *Verfassungslehre*, (Duncker and Humbold, Munich-Leipzig, 1928), p. 208.

10.  Ibid., p.209. J. Freud draws attention to this aspect of Schmitt's thought in his *L'essence du politique*, (Sirey, Paris, 1965), p. 329.

11   J. Habermas, *Strukturwandel der Öffentlichkeit*, (Luchterhand, Neuwied, 1962). The book's central thesis seems to me debatable because in

the whole course of historical analysis no distinction is ever made between the two meanings of 'public', i.e. 'pertaining to the sphere of the state, the *res publica*' (which is the original meaning of the Latin term *publicum*, perpetuated in the classic differentiation between *ius privatum* and *ius publicum*) on the one hand, and 'manifest' (which is the meaning of the term *öffentlich* as opposed to 'secret') on the other.

12  This did not prevent the Enlightenment from having recourse to secret societies as an indispensable instrument for carrying on the fight against absolutism. This subject has been thoroughly researched by R. Koselleck, *Critica illuministica e crisi della società borhgese*, (Il Mulino, Bologna, 1972). On the need for secrecy to combat secret power see below. Thus Kosellek says: 'Against the mysteries of the idolaters of the *arcana* of politics stood the secrecy of the Illuminati. 'Why secret societies?', asks Bode, their champion in North Germany, 'the reply is simple: because it would be madness to play with cards not held close to our chest while our opponents hide their own game.' (p. 108).

13  J.Starobinski, 1789. *Les emblèmes de la raison*, (Flammarion, Paris, 1979), p. 34.

14  I. Kant, 'What is Enlightenment?', in *Kant's Political Writings*, tr. H. B. Nisbet (Cambridge University Press, Cambridge, 1970), p. 55, 59.

15  Ibid., p. 126.

16  Ibid., p. 127.

17  Ibid., p. 128.

18  Cf. *The Republic of Plato*, tr. F. M. Camford, (Oxford University Press, Oxford, 1941), ix 571, pp. 296–7.

19  This quotation is taken from L. Firpo's introduction to T. Tasso, *Tre scritti politici*, (Utet, Turin, 1980), p. 27.

20  The expression derives from Tacitus. For an introduction to the subject cf. F. Meinecke, *Machiavellianism, the Doctrine of Raison d'État and its Place in Modern History*, tr. D. Scott, (Routledge and Kegan Paul, London, 1957), pp. 117 *et seq*.

21  I am quoting from the Amsterdam edition (apud Ludovicum Elzeverium, 1644). The volume contains also, as an introduction, the *Discursus de arcanis rerum publicarum* by Giovanni Corvino, and the *De arcanis rerum publicarum discursus* by Christoph Besold as well as the *De iure publico* also by Clapmar. The passage quoted is on page 10. Both expressions *arcana imperii* and *arcana dominationis* are to be found in Tacitus but without the meanings given them by Clapmar; the first in *Annales*, II 36, and in *Historiae*; the second in *Annales*, II 59.

22  I am quoting the Italian translation (Boringhieri, Turin, 1958), p. 54.

23  The quotation is taken from the edition by J. Poujol, (Librairies d'Agences, Paris, 1961), p. 134.

24  Ibid., p. 139.

25  After writing these pages I came across the book by R. G. Schwarzenberg, *Lo stato spettacolo: Attori e pubblico nel grande teatro della politica mondiale*, (Editori Riuniti, Rome, 1980). The theme of the book is the transformation of political life into a spectacle in which the

leading personalities in political life have to perform like actors. The author's opening words are 'The state is nowadays being transformed into a theatre company, into a producer of spectacles', where the only mistake is the 'nowadays' (moreover, a fairly serious mistake in a book on politics).

26  This is in ch. VI of book III, (Penguin Classics, London, 1970) tr. L. J. Walker, p. 398.

27  An interesting collection of quotations on this subject can be found in R. De Mattei, 'Il problema della "ragion di stato" nel seicento, XIV, Ragion di stato e "mendacio"', *Rivista internazionale di filosofia di diritto*, XXXVII, (1960), pp. 553–76.

28  J. Bodin, *Les six livres de la République* (chez Jacques du Puys, Paris, 1597), vol. IV 6, p. 474 (quoted by De Mattei, *Il problema*, p. 560, n. 27.)

29  M. Foucault, *Discipline and Punish*, tr. A. Sheriden, (Allen Lane, London, 1975), pp. 200–9.

30  Ibid., p. 220.

31  In book 3 of *The Spirit of the Laws* (1748) Montesquieu argues that each type of polity is characterized by a certain 'principle' or ethic: republics by virtue, monarchies by honour and tyrannies by fear. [Ed.]

32  Foucault, *Discipline and Punish*, pp. 224–5.

33  Ibid., p. 225.

34  Cf. Kant, *Political Writings*, tr. H. B. Nisbet (Cambridge University Press, Cambridge, 1970) p. 47. In the republic of Ibania described by the Soviet dissident A. Zivoviev in *Yawning Heights* (The Bodley Head, London, 1979), spying has become the supreme principle of government and is now the general rule not only in the dealings of the government with those it governs, but also between members of the public, so that autocratic power is based not only on its own capacity to spy on its subjects but on the help it is given by those subjects terrorized into spying on each other.

35  Article 616 of the Italian Penal Code makes it a crime, to open another person's correspondence, punishable by a fine or a term of imprisonment, (see S. Borghese, *Il codice penale italiano*, (Milan, 1953, pp. 765–6). This is also upheld in Article 15 of the Constitution. [Ed.]

36  Articles 683–685 of the Italian Penal Code make it a crime, punishable by a fine, to publish without authorization the discussions or secret deliberations of Parliament (C.P. 683) or a criminal court (C.P. 684–5). (Borghese, Il Codice Penale, pp. 882–3). [Ed.]

37  It would be useful to make a distinction between two different functions of secrecy: not revealing a decision because it was not made *by* everyone (a technical secret) and because it is not *for* everyone (a more orthodoxly political secret).

38  *Sottogoverno*, or 'subterranean government', refers to the manner in which Italian parties have brought key ministries and state posts under their own control. Through the creation of special agencies, such as the state oil and gas agency ENI (Ente nazionale idrocarburi), a parallel

administration controlling key economic and welfare services was created, which by-passed the normal civil service. Appointment to these bodies, numbering some 40,000 and affecting all aspects of national and local life, were along party lines and reflected the balance of power between different factions in either central or municipal government. [Ed.]

39 This law simply makes these appointments subject to parliamentary approval. Not surprisingly, this measure has not decreased the dualistic nature of the whole system of 'sottogoverno'. [Ed.]

40 A number of members of the Italian Secret Service were implicated in the Piazza Fontana incident (see ch. 3, note 14). However, they invoked the official secrets act in order to avoid testifying. [Ed.]

41 Michael Confino (ed.), *Daughter of a Revolutionary. Natalie Herzen and the Bakunin-Nechayev Circle*, tr. H. S. Sternberg and L. Bott, (Alcove Press, London, 1974), p. 241: 'The programme can be clearly expressed in a few words: total destruction of the framework of the state and the so-called bourgeois civilization by a spontaneous people's revolution invisibly led, not by an official dictatorship, but by a nameless and collective one, composed of those in favour of total people's liberation from oppression, firmly uniting in a secret society and always and everywhere acting in support of a common aim and in accordance with a common programme.'

## Chapter 5   liberalism old and new

1 The publication details of the books referred to in this paragraph are as follows: E. Cuomo, *Profilo del liberalismo europeo*, (Esi, Rome, 1981); G. Pezzino, *Etica e politica nella crisi liberale*, (Rts, Rome, 1981); N. Boccara, *Vittoriani e radicali. Da Mill a Russell*, (Atanaeo, Rome, 1981); N. Matteuci, *Il liberalismo in una democrazia minacciata*, (Il Mulino, Bologna, 1981); R. Dahrendorf, *La libertà che cambia*, ed. L. Coletti, (Laterza, Bari, 1981); J.-J. Colli, *Liberare la libertà*, (Armando Armando, Rome, 1981). [Tr.]

2 J. S. Mill, *On Liberty*, eds G. Giorello and M. Mondadori, (Il Saggiatore, Milan, 1981).

3 For example, cf. the various comments on this Italian edition of *On Liberty* in the review Pagina, II, 8–9, (May–June 1981), pp. 30–3.

4 Bendetto Croce (1866–1952) was a Neapolitan idealist philosopher of tremendous influence in Italy. A moderate conservative politically, he initially supported Fascism on pragmatic grounds, but after 1924 took a firm stance against it and drafted the 'Protest against the "Manifesto of Fascist Intellectuals"' of 1925. See Richard Bellamy, 'Liberalism and Historicism: Benadetto Croce and the Political Role of Idealism in Modern Italy (1890–1952)', in A. Moulakis (ed.), *The Promise of History*, (Walter de Gruyter, Berlin/New York, 1985), pp. 69–119 for further details. [Ed.]

5  Luigi Salvatorelli (1886–1974) was a democratic-liberal journalist, who wrote for *La Stampa*, and a distinguished and prolific historian. An outspoken critic of Fascism, his books on the Italian Enlightenment and the intellectual origins of the Risorgimento aimed to inspire liberal opposition to the regime. [Ed.]

6  Adolfo Omodeo (1889–1946) was a historian of the medieval Church and restoration Europe. An anti-Fascist, he collaborated with Croce during the late 1920s and 1930s in keeping alive the spirit of nineteenth-century liberalism. After the war he supported the liberal-socialist movement, the Action Party. [Ed.]

7  Piero Gobetti (1901–26) was an extraordinarily precocious intellectual, founding his first review, *Energie Nuove*, in 1918, at the age of seventeen. Although much influenced by Gramsci, he remained a socialistic liberal rather than a communist. In 1922 he set up a weekly, *La rivoluzione liberale*, which became the focus of radical non-communist social and cultural criticism, and opposition to the regime. Many of the contributors admired the English liberal tradition as expressed in the works of Mill and Hobhouse. The edition of Mill's *On Liberty* was reissued at a moment of political crisis (1924), when Mussolini had finally taken the step towards the suppression of opposition political parties. Gobetti himself was forced into exile in Paris, where he died a year later. [Ed.]

8  P. Gobetti, *Scritti politici*, (Einaudi, Turin, 1960), p. 641.

9  Carlo Cattaneo (1801–1869) was a Milanese philosopher of history, economics and linguistics. He had a profound influence on the development of Italian liberalism, supporting a *laissez-faire* economic policy and a federal system for the unification of Italy. An activist in the 1844 Revolution, he was never reconciled to the House of Savoy which ultimately unified the nation. Bobbio has long been interested in his ideas, and edited the three volumes of his philosophical writings. [Ed.]

10  J. S. Mill, 'On Liberty' in M. Warnock (ed.), *Utilitarianism*, (Collins, Glasgow, 1962), p. 202.

11  C. Cattaneo, *Scritti letterari*, (Le Monnier, Florence, 1925), p. 292. I discuss Cattaneo's ideas on this subject more fully in N. Bobbio, *Uno filosofa militante. Studi su Carlo Cattaneo*, (Einaudi, Turin, 1971), in particular pp. 112 *et seq*.

12  F. Stame, 'Oltre Mill' in *Pagina*, II, (May-June 1981), 8–9, p. 30.

13  Mill, *On Liberty*, p. 135.

14  Ibid., p. 205.

15  I am referring especially to the essays contained in N. Bobbio *Dalla struttura alla funzione. Nuovi studi di teoria del diritto*, (Edizioni di Comunità, Milan, 1977).

16  I am referring to the debate surrounding the theses put forward by H. A. L. Hart in his *Law, Liberty and Morality* (Oxford University Press, Oxford, 1963), where he countered the traditionalist ideas of some English judges by explicitly invoking Mill's theories propounded in his essay on liberty.

17  Luigi Einaudi disputed Croce's thesis that liberalism is a 'metapolitical'

doctrine compatible with a number of economic systems, so long as they foster human liberty. Croce's point of view is best expressed in an essay 'Free Enterprise and Liberalism' [Liberismo e liberalismo] (1928) in his *Politics and Morals* (1931), tr. S. J. Castiglione, (George Allen and Unwin, London, 1946), pp. 78–87. Einaudi's two articles, reviewing essays 3–7 of this collection, were originally published in *La riforma sociale* (1928 and 1931 respectively), and are collected in his *Il buongoverno: saggi di economia e politica*, 1897–1954, ed. E. Rossi, (2 vols. Laterza, Bari, 1973), vol. I, pp. 196–228. [Ed.]

18  Hayek makes this claim most forcefully in *Law, Legislation and Liberty*, vol. II: *The Mirage of Social Justice*. (Routledge and Kegan Paul, London, 1976). [Ed.]

19  See Benedetto Croce *The History of Europe in the Nineteenth Century* (1932), tr. H. Furst, (George Allen and Unwin, London, 1934), ch. 1. For an analysis see Richard Bellamy, *Modern Italian Social Theory*, (Cambridge, Polity Press, 1987), ch. 5. [Ed.]

20  Vico's cyclical theory of history, which draws on Polybius' version, is to be found in his *The New Science* (1744), tr. T. Bergin and M. Fisch, (Cornell University Press, Ithaka, 1948). [Ed.]

21  For a typical statement of the thesis of 'overloaded government' see S. Brittan, 'The economic contradictions of democracy', *The British Journal of Political Science*, V, (1975), pp. 129–59. [Ed.]

22  See M. Weber, *The Theory of Social and Economic Organisation*, tr. ed. T. Parsons, (Oxford University Press, New York, 1947), pp. 407–23; and J. Schumpeter, *Capitalism, Socialism and Democracy*, 3rd edn, (George Allen and Unwin, London, 1950), pp. 250–83. The relationship between the two theses is discussed in David Beetham, *Max Weber and the Theory of Modern Politics*, 2nd edn, (Polity Press, Cambridge, 1985), ch. 6. [Ed.]

23  In particular I have in mind the set of articles on the crisis of the Welfare State published in *Mondoperaio*, 4, (1981) with G. Ruffolo's postscript 'Neo-liberalismo e neo-socialismo', pp. 68–71.

24  R. Nozick, *Anarchy, State and Utopia*, (Basil Blackwell, Oxford, 1974). [Ed.]

25  E.g. as in J. Rawls, *A Theory of Justice*, (Clarendon Press, Oxford, 1971). Nozick's book was largely motivated by a criticism of Rawls. [Ed.]

26  Of the many articles contained in the volume *Socialismo liberale e liberalismo sociale*, (Arnoldo Forni, Bologna, 1981), a collection of the papers delivered at a conference held in Milan in December 1979, I would like to draw attention to the one by F. Forte and A. Cassone, 'La terza via per i servizi collettivi' (pp. 393–404), which argues along these lines. (The distinction between social liberalism and liberal socialism goes back to discussions in the 1920s and 1940s between members of the 'Action Party', a non-communist anti-fascist movement made up of liberals and socialists. See editor's preface pp. 2–4. [Ed.])

CHAPTER 6 CONTRACT AND CONTRACTARIANISM IN THE CURRENT
DEBATE

1 In the current debate on contractarianism and neo-contractarianism an
essential text is H. J. S. Maine's famous book *Ancient Law* (1861),
which combines the thesis of the passage of a status society to a contract
society as the process of the breakdown of family relations and the
growth of individualism, with the criticism of unrealistic theories of the
social contract. Pollock, in his comment, argues that Maine's thesis is to
be interpreted as concerning only property law, and hence private law –
see *Ancient Law*, ed. F. Pollock, (Beacon Press, Boston, 1963), p. 422.
2 I discussed this subject more fully in my article '*Diritto privato e diritto
pubblico in Hegel*', in *Studi hegeliani*, (Einaudi, Turin, 1981),
pp. 85–114.
3 R. Polin, *La liberté de notre temps*, (Vrin, Paris, 1977), pp. 216 *et seq*.
4 Article 49 of the Italian Constitution reads as follows: 'All the citizens
have the right to free association in parties for the purpose of competing through democratic procedures to determine the national
policy.' [Ed.]
5 The President of the Republic is elected by a joint session of the Senate
and the Chamber of Deputies, with the participation of the three
delegates from each region. A two-thirds majority is necessary in the first
two ballots, after which an absolute majority suffices. Candidates must
be at least fifty years old and the term of office is seven years. He or she is
a largely ceremonial figure, like the British monarch, though with certain
similar important constitutional functions when no single party or
coalition of parties has a clear majority – an increasingly common
situation in Italy. The following powers are the most important: (i) the
suspensive veto of legislation, (ii) the dissolution of both Houses of
Parliament and (iii) the appointment of the President of the Council of
Ministers. The President of the Council of Ministers performs the role of
the British Prime Minister, and is usually the secretary of the ruling
party, which since 1947 has been the Christian Democrats. Recently
both Spadolini (Republican) and Craxi (Socialist) obtained this office as
leaders of minority parties within a ruling coalition. [Ed.]
6 Cencelli was private secretary to the Christian Democrat press officer,
Adolfo Sarti. His manual provides a mathematical formula whereby a
scale of points are given both to various government positions, from
Prime Minister downwards, and to the relative electoral and parliamentary strengths of the various parties and inter-party positions.
Coalition governments are then formed and the positions distributed
according to these two scales. Although a frequent object of attack, it has
become the basis of most coalition agreements since the first centre-left
groupings of the early 1960s. [Ed.]
7 On the history of the veto on the imperative mandate I have made
considerable use of the information and comments in P. Violante, *Lo*

*spazio della rappresentanza*, (Mozzone, Palermo, 1981), vol. I: *Francia 1788–89*, pp. 29 *et seq*. (plus the footnote to p. 95), 131 *et seq*. and 146 *et seq*.

8 Max Beloff (ed.), *The Federalist*, (Basil Blackwell, Oxford, 1948), p. 45.

9 J. Rawls, *A Theory of Justice*, (Clarendon Press, Oxford, 1972), p. 11.

10 Cf. J. L. Talmon, *The Origins of Totalitarian Democracy*, (Secker and Warburg, London, 1952), p. 103. My attention was drawn to this passage by P. Violante, *Lo spazio della rappresentanza*.

11 E. Burke, *Reflections on the Revolution in France*, (Everyman's Library, New York, 1967), p. 93.

12 This is an allusion to the opening paragraph of the famous 1857 introduction to Marx's *Critique of Political Economy*.

13 i.e. in R. W. and A. J. Carlyle's, *Il pensiero politico medievale*, (Laterza, Bari, 1956), p. 268, a translation of *A History of Medieval Political Thought in the West*, (6 vols, R. Blackwood and Sons, Edinburgh, 1903–36).

14 S. Fragapane, *Contrattualismo e sociologia contemporanea*, (Zanichelli, Bologna, 1892), p. 101.

15 Ibid., p. 99.

## CHAPTER 7 THE RULE OF MEN OR THE RULE OF LAW

1 Bobbio's title does not use 'men' in the generic sense of humanity, but echoes a classical republican formula which contrasts the rule of an all-powerful autocrat with a government restricted by publicly made laws. See, for instance, the words of the Bill of Rights preceding the Constitution of Massachusetts of 1780, which sought to establish 'a government of laws, not of men'. NB The sub-headings in this chapter are the editor's. [Ed.]

2 My inaugural lecture to the Accademia dei Lincei on 26 June 1981 was dedicated to this subject, and subsequently published in *Belfagor*, XXXVII, (1982), pp. 1–12.

3 Plato, *The Laws*, tr. T. J. Saunders, (Penguin, Harmondsworth, rev. edn 1975, 715d, p. 174.

4 Aristotle, *Politics*, tr. T. A. Sinclair, revised by T. J. Saunders, (Penguin, Harmondsworth, 1981), 1286a, p. 221.

5 Plato, 'Statesman', in *The Dialogues of Plato*, tr. B. Jowett, (The Clarendon Press, Oxford, 1892), 294, p. 496–7.

6 Ibid., 296, p. 500.

7 Cf. the famous book by M. Gigante, *Nómos Basileús*, (Arno Press, New York, 1979).

8 Cicero, Pro Cluente, 53. For this and other quotations on the subject of the rule of law cf. F. A. Hayek, *The Constitution of Liberty*, (The University of Chicago Press, Chicago, 1960).

9 Quotation taken from the critical edition by G. E. Woodbine, (Harvard University Press, Harvard, 1968), II, p. 33.

10  I dealt with this topic more fully in N. Bobbio, 'Kelsen e il problema del potere', *Rivista internazionale di filosofia del diritto*, LVIII, (1981), pp. 549–70.

11  Cited from one of the '*Fragments politiques*' in J. J. Rousseau, *Scritti politici*, ed. P. Alatri, (Utet, Turin, 1970), p. 646.

12  For further reflections on this subject see N. Bobbio, 'Dell'uso delle grandi dicotomie nella teoria del diritto', in *Dalla struttura alla funzione. Nuovi studi di teoria del diritto*, (Einaudi di comunità, Milan, 1977), pp. 123–144.

13  St Thomas Aquinas, *Summa Theologica*, Iᵃ, IIᵃᵉ, q. 96. art. 5.

14  A. de Tocqueville, *Democracy in America*, tr. H. Reeve, (Longman, Green, 1875), p. 290.

15  H. von Treitschke, '*Das erste Kaiserreich*' in *Historische und Politische Aufsätze*, (3 vols, S. Hirzel, Leipzig, 4th edn. 1871), vol. 3: *Frankreichs Staatsleben und der Bonapartismus*, p. 110.

16  W. Roscher, *Politik. Geschichtliche Naturlehre der Monarchie, Aristokratie und Demokratie*, (Cotta, Stuttgart, 1892). For more on this subject cf. I. Cervelli, 'Cesarismo, bonapartismo e cavourismo', *La cultura*, X, (1972), pp. 337–91; L. Mangoni, 'Cesarismo, bonapartismo, fascismo', *Studi storici*, n. 3 (1976), pp. 41–61; the entry 'Caesarismus' in O. Brunner *et. al.* (eds), *Geschichtliche Grundbegriffe*, (Kleit Verlag, Stuttgart, 1974), pp. 726–771.

17  Max Beloff (ed.), *The Federalist* (Basil Blackwell, Oxford, 1948), p. 3.

18  *The Political Writings of Leibnitz*, tr. P. Riley (Cambridge University Press, Cambridge, 1972), p. 87.

19  This passage (which is only one of many of the same tenor) I have taken from 'On the Common Saying: "This may be true in theory, but it does not apply in practice"' in *Kant's Political Writings*, tr. H. B. Nisbet (Cambridge University Press, 1970), p. 74.

20  Plato, *The Laws*, 624, p. 45.

21  J. J. Rousseau, 'The Social Contract', in E. Baker (ed.), *Social Contract*, (Oxford University Press, London, 1960), book II 7, p. 205.

22  Taken from the famous last chapter of *The Prince*, tr. W. K. Marriot, (Dent and Sons, London, 1958), ch. XXVI, pp. 145–50.

23  G. W. F. Hegel, *Lectures on the Philosophy of World History. Introduction: Reason in History*, tr. H. B. Nisbet (Cambridge University Press, Cambridge, 1975), pp. 83–4.

24  *Hegel's Philosophy of Right*, tr. T. M. Knox, (Clarendon Press, Oxford, 1942), §§ 93, 102, 380.

25  *Thirteen Epistles of Plato*, tr. L. A. Post, (Clarendon Press, Oxford, 1925), p. 65, Seventh Epistle, 326ab.

26  F. Neumann, *The Democratic and the Authoritarian State*, (Collier-Macmillan, London, 1957), p. 241 *et seq*.

27  A. Gramsci, *Prison Notebooks*, tr. Q. Hoare and G. N. Smith, (Lawrence and Wishart, London, 1971), p. 219.

28  M. Weber, *Economy and Society*, eds G. Roth and C. Wittich, (University of California Press, Berkeley, 1978), vol. I, pp. 442–3.

# Index

Clapmar, A. 86
*clientelismo* 36
Cole, G. D. H. 8, 18, 50
Colletti, Lucio 99
Colli, Jean-Claude 99
Commune *see* Paris Commune
communism *see* Marxism; Eastern
  bloc
Communist Party (Italian) 3, 71, 78,
  164
'computer-ocracy' 31, 34, 54, 97
consensus in a democracy 61–2, 119
conspiracy 88–9
Constant, Benjamin 104
constitutionalism 123–5, 142
constitution (Italian) *see* Italy,
  Constitution
contractarianism 10, 11, 13, 27, 116–
  17, 118–37 *passim*, 171
corporatism 28, 50, 71, 163
*coup d'état* 88, 154
Croce, Benedetto 99, 108, 110, 168,
  170
cryptogovernment 95–7
Cuomo, Ettore 98

Dahl, R. A. 5, 7–9
Dahrendorf, Ralf 31, 44, 72, 161
decentralization 82
demands made on government *see*
  overloading
democracy
  broken promises 8, 18–19, 26–41
    *passim*
  as a bourgeois ideology 49, 78, 133
  classical *see* democracy, Greek
  communist concept of 78
  compared to autocracy 9, 31, 39,
    40, 93
  compared to despotism 17, 20, 34,
    56, 59, 62, 111, 146–8
  competitive model 5–6
  consociational 40
  constraints of 63–78 *passim*
  and contract theory *see* contrac-
    tarianism
  contrasted with dictatorship 71,
    81; *see also* dictatorship
  contrasted with fanaticism 41

  contrasted with totalitarianism 40,
    44, 61, 73
  democratic state compared with
    non-democratic state 18, 41–2,
    55–6; *see also* state
  direct 5, 8, 14, 17, 20, 32, 43–62
    *passim*
  in Eastern Europe *see* Eastern
    bloc
  equitable principles of 102
  failures of 79; *see also* democracy,
    broken promises
  future of 23–42 *passim*, 72
  Greek 17, 29, 33, 44, 53, 58, 60,
    73, 80, 89, 120, 138–41, 149;
    *see also* Plato
  minimal definition 5, 19, 24–6, 40
  modern contrasted with classical
    *see* democracy, Greek
  paradoxes of 79, 93
  participatory *see* democracy, direct
  plebiscitary 155
  political and social democracy
    54–5
  relationship to bureaucracy 38; *see*
    *also* bureaucracy
  relationship to individualism 27
  relationship to liberalism 4–5, 10,
    21, 25–6, 31, 39, 99–117
    *passim*
  relationship to oligarchy *see*
    oligarchy
  relationship to parliamentarian-
    ism 45–6, 55, 67
  relationship to pluralism *see*
    pluralism
  relationship to technocracy *see*
    technocracy
  representative 20, 29, 31, 46;
    contrasted with direct 17, 43–62
    *passim*; compared with
    parliamentary state 45–8
  role of parties in 5, 14
  role of secrecy in *see* invisible
    power
  rules of 19, 24–5, 41–2, 62, 63–7,
    69–70, 78, 156
  transformations of *see* trans-
    formations